Proverbs

A LIFE APPLICATION® BIBLE STUDY

Part 1:

Complete text of Proverbs with study notes from the *Life Application Bible*

Part 2:

Thirteen lessons for individual or group study

Study questions written and edited by
REV. NEIL S. WILSON
DR. JAMES C. GALVIN
REV. DAVID R. VEERMAN
DR. BRUCE B. BARTON

Tyndale House Publishers, Inc.
Wheaton, Illinois

Life Application Bible Studies

Genesis TLB
Joshua TLB
Judges NIV
Ruth & Esther TLB
1 Samuel NIV
Ezra & Nehemiah NIV
Proverbs NIV
Daniel NIV
Hosea & Jonah TLB
Matthew NIV
Mark TLB & NIV
Luke NIV
John NIV
Acts TLB & NIV
Romans NIV
1 Corinthians NIV
2 Corinthians NIV
Galatians & Ephesians NIV
Philippians & Colossians NIV
1 & 2 Timothy & Titus NIV
1 & 2 Thessalonians & Philemon NIV
Hebrews NIV
1 & 2 Peter & Jude NIV
James NIV
1 & 2 & 3 John NIV
Revelation NIV

ISBN 0-8423-2737-1

Printed in the United States of America

00 99
13 12 11 10 9

NOTES

In addition to providing the reader with many application notes, the *Life Application Bible* offers several explanatory notes that help the reader understand culture, history, context, difficult-to-understand passages, background, places, theological concepts, and the relationship of various passages in Scripture to other passages.

BOOK INTRODUCTION

The Book Introduction is divided into several easy-to-find parts:

Timeline. A guide that puts the Bible book into its historical setting. It lists the key events and the dates when they occurred.

Vital Statistics. A list of straight facts about the book—those pieces of information you need to know at a glance.

Overview. A summary of the book with general lessons and applications that can be learned from the book as a whole.

Blueprint. The outline of the book. It is printed in easy-to-understand language and is designed for easy memorization. To the right of each main heading is a key lesson that is taught in that particular section.

Megathemes. A section that gives the main themes of the Bible book, explains their significance, and then tells why they are still important for us today.

Map. If included, this shows the key places found in that book and retells the story of the book from a geographical perspective.

OUTLINE

The *Life Application Bible* has a new, custom-made outline that was designed specifically from an application point of view. Several unique features should be noted:

1. To avoid confusion and to aid memory work, the book outline has only three levels for headings. Main outline heads are marked with a capital letter. Subheads are marked by a number. Minor explanatory heads have no letter or number.

2. Each main outline head marked by a letter also has a brief paragraph below it summarizing the Bible text and offering a general application.

3. Parallel passages are listed where they apply.

PERSONALITY PROFILES
Another unique feature of this Bible is the profiles of key Bible people, including their strengths and weaknesses, greatest accomplishments and mistakes, and key lessons from their lives.

MAPS
The *Life Application Bible* has a thorough and comprehensive Bible atlas built right into the book. There are two kinds of maps: A book introduction map, telling the story of the book, and thumbnail maps in the notes, plotting most geographic movements.

CHARTS AND DIAGRAMS
Many charts and diagrams are included to help the reader better visualize difficult concepts or relationships. Most charts not only present the needed information, but show the significance of the information as well.

CROSS REFERENCES
An updated, exhaustive cross-reference system in the margins of the Bible text helps the reader find related passages quickly.

TEXTUAL NOTES
Directly related to the text of the New International Version, the textual notes provide explanations on certain wording in the translation, alternate translations, and information about readings in the ancient manuscripts.

HIGHLIGHTED NOTES
In each Bible study lesson you will be asked to read specific notes as part of your preparation. These notes have been highlighted by a bullet (•) so that you can find them easily.

PROVERBS

PROVERBS

VITAL STATISTICS

PURPOSE:
To teach people how to attain wisdom and discipline and a prudent life, and to do what is right and just and fair (see 1:2, 3)—in short, to apply divine wisdom to daily life and to provide moral instruction

AUTHOR:
Solomon wrote most of this book, with Agur and Lemuel contributing some of the later sections

DATE WRITTEN:
Solomon wrote and compiled most of these proverbs early in his reign

SETTING:
This is a book of wise sayings, a textbook for teaching people how to live godly lives through the repetition of wise thoughts

KEY VERSE:
"The fear of the LORD is the beginning of knowledge, but fools despise wisdom and discipline" (1:7).

SPECIAL FEATURES:
The book uses varied *literary forms:* poems, brief parables, pointed questions, and couplets. Other *literary devices* include antithesis, comparison, and personification.

ALPHABET, letters, vowels, and consonants, formed into words, sentences, paragraphs, and books—spoken, lectured, signed, whispered, written, and printed. From friendly advice to impassioned speeches and from dusty volumes to daily tabloids, messages are sent and received with each sender trying to impart knowledge . . . and wisdom.

Woven into human fabric is the desire to learn and understand. Our minds set us apart from animals, and we analyze, conceptualize, theorize, discuss, and debate everything from science to the supernatural. And we build schools, institutes, and universities where learned professors can teach us about the world and about life.

Knowledge is good, but there is a vast difference between "knowledge" (having the facts) and "wisdom" (applying those facts to life). We may amass knowledge, but without wisdom, our knowledge is useless. We must learn how to *live out* what we know.

The wisest man who ever lived, Solomon, left us a legacy of written wisdom in three volumes—Proverbs, Ecclesiastes, and Song of Songs. In these books, under the inspiration of the Holy Spirit, he gives practical insights and guidelines for life.

In the first of these three volumes, Solomon passes on his practical advice in the form of proverbs. A proverb is a short, concise sentence which conveys moral truth. The book of Proverbs is a collection of these wise statements. The main theme of Proverbs, as we might expect, is the nature of true wisdom. Solomon writes, "The fear of the LORD is the beginning of knowledge, but fools despise wisdom and discipline" (1:7). He then proceeds to give hundreds of practical examples of how to live according to godly wisdom.

Proverbs covers a wide range of topics, including youth and discipline, family life, self-control and resisting temptation, business matters, words and the tongue, knowing God, marriage, seeking the truth, wealth and poverty, immorality, and, of course, wisdom. These proverbs are short poems (usually in couplet form), containing a holy mixture of common sense and timely warnings. Although they are not meant to teach doctrine, a person who follows their advice will walk closely with God. The word "proverb" comes from a Hebrew word which means "to rule or to govern," and these sayings, reminders, and admonitions provide profound advice for governing our lives.

As you read Proverbs, understand that knowing God is the key to wisdom. Listen to the thoughts and lessons from the world's wisest man, and apply these truths to your life. Don't just read these proverbs, act on them!

THE BLUEPRINT

A. WISDOM FOR YOUNG PEOPLE (1:1—9:18)	Solomon instructed the young people of his day like a father giving advice to his child. While many of these proverbs are directed toward young people, the principles supporting them are helpful to all believers, male and female, young and old. Anyone beginning their journey to discover more of wisdom will benefit greatly from these wise sayings.
B. WISDOM FOR ALL PEOPLE (10:1—24:34)	Solomon wanted to impart wisdom to all people, regardless of their age, sex, or position in society. These short, wise sayings give us practical wisdom for daily living. We should study them diligently and integrate them into our lives.
C. WISDOM FOR THE LEADERS (25:1—31:31)	In addition to the proverbs which Solomon collected, the men of Hezekiah collected many proverbs that Solomon and others wrote. While most of these are general in nature, many are directed specifically to the king and those who dealt with the king. These are particularly useful for those who are leaders or aspire to be leaders.

MEGATHEMES

THEME	EXPLANATION	IMPORTANCE
Wisdom	God wants his people to be wise. Two kinds of people portray two contrasting paths of life. The fool is the wicked, stubborn person who hates or ignores God. The wise person seeks to know and love God.	When we choose God's way, he grants us wisdom. His Word, the Bible, leads us to live rightly, have right relationships, and make right decisions.
Relationships	Proverbs gives us advice for developing our personal relationships with friends, family members, and co-workers. In every relationship, we must show love, dedication, and high moral standards.	To relate to people, we need consistency, tact, and discipline to use the wisdom God gives us. If we don't treat others according to the wisdom God gives, our relationships will suffer.
Speech	What we say shows our real attitude toward others. How we talk reveals what we're really like. Our speech is a test of how wise we have become.	To be wise in our speech we need to use self-control. Our words should be honest and well-chosen.
Work	God controls the final outcome of all we do. We are accountable to carry out our work with diligence and discipline, not laziness.	Because God evaluates how we live, we should work purposefully. We must never be lax or self-satisfied in using our skills.
Success	Although people work very hard for money and fame, God views success as having a good reputation, moral character, and the spiritual devotion to obey him.	A successful relationship with God counts for eternity. Everything else is perishable. All our resources, time, and talents come from God. We should strive to use them wisely.

A. WISDOM FOR YOUNG PEOPLE (1:1 – 9:18)

Proverbs begins with a clear statement of its purpose – to impart wisdom for godly living. The first few chapters are Solomon's fatherly advice to young people. Although most of the material in this section is directed toward young people, all who seek wisdom will greatly benefit from these wise words. This is where one can discover the source of wisdom, the value of wisdom, and the benefits of wisdom.

Prologue: Purpose and Theme

1 The proverbs of Solomon son of David, king of Israel:

[2]for attaining wisdom and discipline;
for understanding words of insight;
[3]for acquiring a disciplined and prudent life,
doing what is right and just and fair;
[4]for giving prudence to the simple,
knowledge and discretion to the young –
[5]let the wise listen and add to their learning,
and let the discerning get guidance –
[6]for understanding proverbs and parables,
the sayings and riddles of the wise.

[7]The fear of the LORD is the beginning of knowledge,
but fools[a] despise wisdom and discipline.

1:1 1 Kgs 4:32; Prov 25:1
1:2 Prov 4:5; 7:4
1:3 Prov 2:9
1:4 Prov 8:4; 9:4
1:7 Prov 9:10; 15:33

Exhortations to Embrace Wisdom

Warning Against Enticement

[8]Listen, my son, to your father's instruction
and do not forsake your mother's teaching.
[9]They will be a garland to grace your head
and a chain to adorn your neck.

[10]My son, if sinners entice you,
do not give in to them.
[11]If they say, "Come along with us;
let's lie in wait for someone's blood,

1:10 Ps 1:1; Prov 7:21

[a] 7 The Hebrew words rendered *fool* in Proverbs, and often elsewhere in the Old Testament, denote one who is morally deficient.

• **1:1** What the book of Psalms is to devotional life, the book of Proverbs is to everyday life. Proverbs gives practical suggestions for effective living. This book is not just a collection of homey sayings; it contains deep spiritual insights drawn from experience. A *proverb* is a short, wise, easy-to-learn saying that calls a person to action. It doesn't argue about basic spiritual and moral beliefs; it assumes we already hold them. The book of Proverbs focuses on God – his character, works, and blessings – and it tells how we can live in close relationship to him.

1:1 Solomon, the third king of Israel, son of the great King David, reigned during Israel's golden age. When God said he would give him whatever he wanted, he asked for a discerning heart (1 Kings 3:5–14). God was pleased with this request, and he not only made Solomon wise but also gave him great riches, power, and peace. Solomon built the glorious temple in Jerusalem (1 Kings 6) and wrote most of the book of Proverbs. His Profile is found in 1 Kings 3.

1:6 "Riddles" were thought-provoking questions.

• **1:7** One of the most annoying types of people is a know-it-all, a person who has a dogmatic opinion about everything, is closed to anything new, resents discipline, and refuses to learn. Solomon calls this kind of person a fool. Don't be a know-it-all. Instead, be open to the advice of others, especially those who know you well and can give valuable insight and counsel. Learn how to learn from others. Remember, only God knows it all.

• **1:7–9** In this age of information, knowledge is plentiful, but wisdom is scarce. Wisdom means far more than simply knowing a lot. It is a basic attitude that affects every aspect of life. The foundation of knowledge is to fear the Lord – to honor and respect God, to live in awe of his power. Faith in God should be the controlling principle for your understanding of the world, your attitudes, and your actions. Trust in God, and he will make you truly wise.

• **1:8** Our actions speak louder than our words. This is especially true in the home. Children learn values, morals, and priorities by observing how their parents act and react every day. If parents exhibit a deep reverence for and dependence on God, the children will catch these attitudes. Let them see your reverence for God. Teach them right living by giving worship an important place in your family life and by reading the Bible together.

1:10–19 Sin is enticing because it offers a quick route to prosperity and makes us feel like one of the crowd. When we go along with others and refuse to listen to the truth, our own appetites become our masters, and we'll do anything to satisfy them. But sin, even when attractive, is deadly. We must learn to make choices, not on the basis of flashy appeal or short-range pleasure, but in view of the long-range effects. Sometimes this means steering clear of people who want to entice us into activities that we know are wrong. We can't be friendly with sin and expect our lives to remain unaffected.

let's waylay some harmless soul;
[12]let's swallow them alive, like the grave,[a]
and whole, like those who go down to the pit;
[13]we will get all sorts of valuable things
and fill our houses with plunder;
[14]throw in your lot with us,
and we will share a common purse"—
[15]my son, do not go along with them,
do not set foot on their paths;
[16]for their feet rush into sin,
they are swift to shed blood.
[17]How useless to spread a net
in full view of all the birds!
[18]These men lie in wait for their own blood;
they waylay only themselves!
[19]Such is the end of all who go after ill-gotten gain;
it takes away the lives of those who get it.

1:15 Ps 1:1; 26:4 2 Cor 6:17
1:16 Prov 4:16
1:18 Prov 5:22
1:19 Prov 15:27 28:25

Warning Against Rejecting Wisdom

[20]Wisdom calls aloud in the street,
she raises her voice in the public squares;
[21]at the head of the noisy streets[b] she cries out,
in the gateways of the city she makes her speech:

[22]"How long will you simple ones[c] love your simple ways?
How long will mockers delight in mockery
and fools hate knowledge?
[23]If you had responded to my rebuke,
I would have poured out my heart to you
and made my thoughts known to you.
[24]But since you rejected me when I called
and no one gave heed when I stretched out my hand,

1:22 Prov 9:4; 14:15
1:24 Prov 15:32 Isa 65:12; 66:4

[a] 12 Hebrew *Sheol* [b] 21 Hebrew; Septuagint / *on the tops of the walls* [c] 22 The Hebrew word rendered *simple* in Proverbs generally denotes one without moral direction and inclined to evil.

UNDERSTANDING PROVERBS Most often, proverbs are written in the form of couplets. These are constructed in three ways:

Type	*Description*	*Key Word(s)*	*Examples*
Contrasting	Meaning and application come from the difference or contrast between the two statements of the proverb	"but"	10:6; 15:25, 27
Comparing	Meaning and application come from the similarities or comparison between the two statements of the proverb	"as/so" "better/than"	10:26; 15:16, 17
Complementing	Meaning and application come from the way the second statement complements the first	"and"	10:18; 15:23

1:19 Going after "ill-gotten gain" is one of Satan's surest traps. It begins when he plants the suggestion that we can't live without some possession or more money. Then that desire fans its own fire until it becomes an all-consuming obsession. Ask God for wisdom to recognize any greedy desire before it destroys you. God will help you overcome it (1:23).

1:20 The picture of wisdom calling aloud in the streets is a personification—a literary device to make wisdom come alive for us. Wisdom is not a separate being; it is the mind of God revealed. By reading about Jesus Christ's earthly ministry, we can see wisdom in action. In order to understand how to become wise, we can listen to wisdom calling and instructing us in the book of Proverbs (see the chart in chapter 14). For New Testament calls to wisdom, see 2 Timothy 1:7 and James 1:5. Make sure you don't reject God's offer of wisdom to you.

• **1:22** In the book of Proverbs, a "simple one" or a fool is not someone with a *mental* deficiency but someone with a *character* deficiency (such as rebellion, laziness, or anger). The fool is not stupid, but is unable to tell right from wrong or good from bad.

1:23–28 God is more than willing to pour out his heart and make known his thoughts to us. To receive his advice, we must be willing to listen, refusing to let pride stand in our way. Pride is thinking more highly of our own wisdom and desires than of God's. If we think we know better than God or feel we have no need of God's direction, we have fallen into foolish and disastrous pride.

[25]since you ignored all my advice
and would not accept my rebuke,
[26]I in turn will laugh at your disaster;
I will mock when calamity overtakes you—
[27]when calamity overtakes you like a storm,
when disaster sweeps over you like a whirlwind,
when distress and trouble overwhelm you.

[28]"Then they will call to me but I will not answer;
they will look for me but will not find me.
[29]Since they hated knowledge
and did not choose to fear the LORD,
[30]since they would not accept my advice
and spurned my rebuke,
[31]they will eat the fruit of their ways
and be filled with the fruit of their schemes.
[32]For the waywardness of the simple will kill them,
and the complacency of fools will destroy them;
[33]but whoever listens to me will live in safety
and be at ease, without fear of harm."

1:25 2 Chron 36:16
1:27 Prov 3:25; 10:25
1:28 Job 27:9; Ezek 8:18
1:31 Job 4:8; Prov 5:22; 22:8
1:33 Prov 3:24-26

Moral Benefits of Wisdom

2 My son, if you accept my words
and store up my commands within you,
[2]turning your ear to wisdom
and applying your heart to understanding,
[3]and if you call out for insight
and cry aloud for understanding,
[4]and if you look for it as for silver
and search for it as for hidden treasure,
[5]then you will understand the fear of the LORD
and find the knowledge of God.
[6]For the LORD gives wisdom,
and from his mouth come knowledge and understanding.
[7]He holds victory in store for the upright,
he is a shield to those whose walk is blameless,
[8]for he guards the course of the just
and protects the way of his faithful ones.

[9]Then you will understand what is right and just
and fair—every good path.
[10]For wisdom will enter your heart,
and knowledge will be pleasant to your soul.

2:1 Prov 3:1; 4:10
2:4 Mt 13:44
2:6 Jas 1:5
2:9 Prov 1:2-6
2:10 Prov 14:33

•**1:31, 32** Many proverbs point out that the "fruit of their ways" will be the consequences people will experience in this life. Faced with either choosing God's wisdom or persisting in rebellious independence, many decide to go it alone. The problems such people create for themselves will destroy them. Don't ignore God's advice even if it is painful for the present. It will keep you from greater pain in the future.

2:3–6 Wisdom is both a God-given gift and the fruit of an energetic search. Wisdom's starting point is God and his revealed Word, the source of "knowledge and understanding" (2:6). In that sense, it is his gift to us. But he gives it only to those who earnestly seek it. The pathway to wisdom is strenuous. When we are on it, we discover that true wisdom is God's and that we cannot create it by our own efforts. But because God's wisdom is hidden from the rebellious and foolish, it takes effort to find it and use it.

2:6, 7 God gives us wisdom and victory, but not for drifting through life or acting irresponsibly with his gifts and resources. If we are faithful and keep our purpose in life clearly in mind, he will keep us from pride and greed.

•**2:9, 10** We gain wisdom through a constant process of growing. First, we must trust and honor God. Second, we must realize that the Bible reveals God's wisdom to us. Third, we must make a lifelong series of right choices. Fourth, when we make sinful or mistaken choices, we must learn from our errors and recover. People don't develop all aspects of wisdom at once. For example, some people have more insight than discretion; others have more knowledge than common sense. But we can pray for all aspects of wisdom and take the steps to develop them in our lives.

2:11 Discretion is the ability to tell right from wrong. It enables the believer to detect evil motives in men (2:12) and women (2:16). With practice it helps us evaluate courses of action and consequences. For some it is a gift; for most it is developed by using

[11]Discretion will protect you,
and understanding will guard you.

[12]Wisdom will save you from the ways of wicked men,
from men whose words are perverse,
[13]who leave the straight paths
to walk in dark ways,
[14]who delight in doing wrong
and rejoice in the perverseness of evil,
[15]whose paths are crooked
and who are devious in their ways.

[16]It will save you also from the adulteress,
from the wayward wife with her seductive words,
[17]who has left the partner of her youth
and ignored the covenant she made before God.[a]
[18]For her house leads down to death
and her paths to the spirits of the dead.
[19]None who go to her return
or attain the paths of life.

[20]Thus you will walk in the ways of good men
and keep to the paths of the righteous.

2:13 Prov 4:19
2:14 Prov 10:23
2:16 Prov 6:24; 23:27
2:20 Prov 13:20

[a] 17 Or *covenant of her God*

PEOPLE CALLED "WISE" IN THE BIBLE
The special description "wise" is used for 12 significant people in the Bible. They can be helpful models in our own pursuit of wisdom.

The Person	*Their Role*	*Reference*	*How they practiced wisdom*
Joseph	Wise leader	Acts 7:10	Prepared for a major famine. Helped rule Egypt.
Moses	Wise leader	Acts 7:20–22	Learned all the Egyptian wisdom, then graduated to God's lessons in wisdom to lead Israel out of Egypt.
Bezalel	Wise artist	Exodus 31:1–5	Designed and supervised the construction of the tabernacle and its utensils in the desert.
Joshua	Wise leader	Deuteronomy 34:9	Learned by observing Moses, obeyed God, led the people into the promised land.
David	Wise leader	2 Samuel 14:20	Never let his failures keep him from the source of wisdom—reverence for God.
Abigail	Wise wife	1 Samuel 25:3	Managed her household well in spite of a surly and mean husband.
Solomon	Wise leader	1 Kings 3:5–14; 4:29–34	Knew what to do even though he often failed to put his own wisdom into action.
Daniel	Wise counselor	Daniel 5:11, 12	Known as a man in touch with God. A solver of complex problems with God's help
Magi	Wise learners	Matthew 2:1–12	Not only received special knowledge of God's visit to earth, but checked it out personally.
Stephen	Wise leader	Acts 6:8–10	Organized the distribution of food to the Grecian widows. Preached the gospel to the Jews.
Paul	Wise messenger	2 Peter 3:15, 16	Spent his life communicating God's love to all who would listen.
Christ	Wise youth Wise Savior Wisdom of God	Luke 2:40, 52; 1 Corinthians 1:20–25	Not only lived a perfect life, but died on the cross to save us and make God's wise plan of eternal life available to us.

God's truth to make wise choices day by day. Hebrews 5:14 emphasizes that we must train ourselves in order to have discretion.

2:16, 17 An *adulteress* is a seductive woman or a prostitute. Two of the most difficult sins to resist are pride and sexual immorality. Both are seductive. Pride says, "I deserve it"; sexual desire says, "I need it." In combination, their appeal is deadly. In fact, says Solomon, only by relying on God's strength can we overcome them. Pride appeals to the empty head; sexual enticement to the empty heart. By looking to God, we can fill our heads with his wisdom and our hearts with his love. Don't be fooled – remember what God says about who you are and what you were meant to be. Ask him for strength to resist these temptations.

[21]For the upright will live in the land,
and the blameless will remain in it;
[22]but the wicked will be cut off from the land,
and the unfaithful will be torn from it.

2:21 Prov 10:30
2:22 Deut 28:63

Further Benefits of Wisdom

3 My son, do not forget my teaching,
but keep my commands in your heart,
[2]for they will prolong your life many years
and bring you prosperity.

[3]Let love and faithfulness never leave you;
bind them around your neck,
write them on the tablet of your heart.
[4]Then you will win favor and a good name
in the sight of God and man.

[5]Trust in the LORD with all your heart
and lean not on your own understanding;
[6]in all your ways acknowledge him,
and he will make your paths straight.[a]

[7]Do not be wise in your own eyes;
fear the LORD and shun evil.
[8]This will bring health to your body
and nourishment to your bones.

[9]Honor the LORD with your wealth,
with the firstfruits of all your crops;
[10]then your barns will be filled to overflowing,
and your vats will brim over with new wine.

[11]My son, do not despise the LORD's discipline
and do not resent his rebuke,
[12]because the LORD disciplines those he loves,
as a father[b] the son he delights in.

3:1 Ps 119:93 Prov 9:11; 10:27
3:2 Prov 6:21; 7:3
3:4 Prov 8:35
3:7 Job 1:1; 28:28 Prov 4:21; 8:13 16:6
3:9 Ex 23:19 Prov 11:24 19:17 Joel 2:24 Mal 3:10
3:11 Job 5:17 Ps 94:12 Prov 13:24

[a] *6 Or will direct your paths* [b] *12* Hebrew; Septuagint / *and he punishes*

3:3 Two important character qualities are love and faithfulness. Both involve actions as well as attitudes. A loving person not only feels love; he also acts loyally and responsibly. A faithful person not only believes the truth; he also works for justice for others. Thoughts and words are not enough—our lives reveal whether we are truly loving and faithful.

3:5, 6 When we have an important decision to make, we sometimes feel that we can't trust anyone—not even God. But God knows what is best for us. He is a better judge of what we want than even we are! We must trust him completely in every choice we make. We should not omit careful thinking or belittle our God-given ability to reason; but we should not trust our own ideas to the exclusion of all others. We must not be wise in our own eyes. We should always be willing to listen to and be corrected by God's Word and wise counselors. Bring your decisions to God in prayer; use the Bible as your guide; and then follow God's leading. He will make your paths straight by both guiding and protecting you.

• **3:6** To receive God's guidance, said Solomon, we must acknowledge God in all our ways. About a thousand years later, Jesus emphasized this same truth (Matthew 6:33). Look at your values and priorities. What is important to you? In what areas have you not acknowledged him? What is his advice? In many areas of your life you may already acknowledge God, but it is in the areas where you attempt to restrict or ignore his influence that will cause you grief. Make him a vital part of everything you do; then he will guide you because you will be working to accomplish his purposes.

3:9, 10 The *firstfruits* refers to the practice of giving to God's use the first and best portion of the harvest (Deuteronomy 26:9–11). Many people give God their leftovers. If they can afford to donate anything, they do so. These people may be sincere and contribute willingly, but their attitude is nonetheless backward. It is better to give God the first part of our income. This demonstrates that God has first place in our lives and that our resources belong to him. Giving to God first helps us conquer greed, helps us properly manage God's resources, and opens us to God's blessings.

3:11, 12 *Discipline* means "to teach and to train." Discipline sounds negative to many people because some disciplinarians are not loving. God, however, is the source of all love. He doesn't punish us because he enjoys inflicting pain but because he is deeply concerned about our development. He knows that in order to become morally strong and good, we must learn the difference between right and wrong. His loving discipline enables us to do this.

3:11, 12 It's difficult to know when God has been disciplining us until we look back on the situation later. Not every calamity comes directly from God, of course. But if we rebel against God and refuse to repent when he has identified some sin in our lives, God may use guilt, crises, or bad experiences to bring us back to him. Sometimes, however, difficult times come even when there is no flagrant sin in our lives. Our response then should be patience, integrity, and trust that God will show us what to do.

3:13
Prov 8:10,34

13Blessed is the man who finds wisdom,
the man who gains understanding,
14for she is more profitable than silver
and yields better returns than gold.
15She is more precious than rubies;
nothing you desire can compare with her.

3:16,17
Prov 16:7; 22:4

16Long life is in her right hand;
in her left hand are riches and honor.
17Her ways are pleasant ways,
and all her paths are peace.

3:18
Prov 11:30

18She is a tree of life to those who embrace her;
those who lay hold of her will be blessed.

19By wisdom the LORD laid the earth's foundations,
by understanding he set the heavens in place;
20by his knowledge the deeps were divided,
and the clouds let drop the dew.

3:21
Prov 4:21; 9:11

21My son, preserve sound judgment and discernment,
do not let them out of your sight;
22they will be life for you,
an ornament to grace your neck.

3:23
Ps 37:23; 91:11
Prov 4:12; 10:9

23Then you will go on your way in safety,
and your foot will not stumble;
24when you lie down, you will not be afraid;
when you lie down, your sleep will be sweet.
25Have no fear of sudden disaster
or of the ruin that overtakes the wicked,

WISDOM: APPLIED TRUTH
The book of Proverbs tells us about people who have wisdom and enjoy its benefits.

Reference	*The Person who has Wisdom*	*Benefits of Wisdom*
Proverbs 3; 4 A father's instructions	Is loving Is faithful Trusts in the Lord Puts God first Turns away from evil Knows right from wrong Listens and learns Does what is right	Long, prosperous life Favor with God and people Reputation for good judgment Success Health, vitality Riches, honor, pleasure, peace Protection
Proverbs 8; 9 Wisdom speaks	Possesses knowledge and discretion Hates pride, arrogance, and evil behavior Respects and fears God Gives good advice and has common sense Loves and is teachable Knows God	Riches, honor Justice Righteousness Life God's favor Constant learning Understanding

3:13–15 How do people become successful in their family life, in business, or in athletics? By hard work and consistent discipline. The Christian life is much the same. Some people think it's too difficult, but achieving anything worthwhile requires hard work. Being a Christian is not a shortcut to an easy life. When you search for wisdom, working hard at living as God asks, you discover that no worldly success can compare with the joy of knowing God.

• **3:16, 17** Proverbs contains many strong statements about the benefits of wisdom, including long life, wealth, honor, and peace. If you aren't experiencing them, does this mean you are short on wisdom? Not necessarily. Instead of guarantees, these statements are general principles to make us think. In a perfect world, wise behavior would always lead to these benefits. Even in our troubled world, living wisely usually results in obvious blessings – but not always. Sometimes sin intervenes, and the blessings must be delayed until Jesus returns to establish his eternal kingdom. That is why we must "live by faith, not by sight" (2 Corinthians 5:7). We can be sure that wisdom ultimately leads to blessing.

3:21 What is the difference between sound judgment and discernment? Discernment (or discretion) is the ability God gives to many people to think and make correct choices. Sound judgment, however, he gives only to those who follow him. Sound judgment includes discernment, but goes beyond it. It also includes the knowledge that comes from instruction, training, and discipline, and the insight that results from knowing and applying God's truths.

[26]for the LORD will be your confidence
and will keep your foot from being snared.

[27]Do not withhold good from those who deserve it,
when it is in your power to act.
[28]Do not say to your neighbor,
"Come back later; I'll give it tomorrow"—
when you now have it with you.

[29]Do not plot harm against your neighbor,
who lives trustfully near you.
[30]Do not accuse a man for no reason—
when he has done you no harm.

[31]Do not envy a violent man
or choose any of his ways,
[32]for the LORD detests a perverse man
but takes the upright into his confidence.

[33]The LORD's curse is on the house of the wicked,
but he blesses the home of the righteous.
[34]He mocks proud mockers
but gives grace to the humble.
[35]The wise inherit honor,
but fools he holds up to shame.

3:29 Ps 35:20; 55:20 Prov 14:22
3:30 Prov 18:6 Rom 12:18
3:31 Ps 37:11; 73:3 Prov 23:17
3:32 Prov 6:16; 11:20
3:34 Jas 4:6

Wisdom Is Supreme

4 Listen, my sons, to a father's instruction;
pay attention and gain understanding.
[2]I give you sound learning,
so do not forsake my teaching.
[3]When I was a boy in my father's house,
still tender, and an only child of my mother,
[4]he taught me and said,
"Lay hold of my words with all your heart;
keep my commands and you will live.
[5]Get wisdom, get understanding;
do not forget my words or swerve from them.
[6]Do not forsake wisdom, and she will protect you;
love her, and she will watch over you.

4:1 Prov 1:8; 5:1 6:20
4:4 Prov 3:1; 4:10 9:11
4:6 Prov 3:26 8:14,17 2 Thess 2:10

3:27, 28 Delaying to do good is inconsiderate and unfair. Whether it is repaying a loan, returning a tool, or fulfilling a promise, withholding destroys trust and creates a great inconvenience. Be as eager to do good as you are to have good done to you.

3:30 This verse implies that there is a time for quarreling and fighting. Injustice must be combated, sin resisted, and evil confronted wherever it appears. But don't waste time and energy on arguments over trivial matters or personal inconvenience. Save your energy for the real battles against sin and God's enemies.

4:3, 4 One of the greatest responsibilities of parents is to encourage their children to become wise. Here Solomon tells how his father, David, encouraged him to seek after wisdom when he was young ("tender") (see 1 Kings 2:1–9 and 1 Chronicles 28, 29 for David's full charge to his son). This encouragement may have prompted Solomon to ask God for a discerning heart above everything else (1 Kings 3:9). Wisdom can be passed on from parents to children, from generation to generation. Ultimately, of course, all wisdom comes from God; parents can only urge their children to turn to him. If your parents never taught you in this way, God's Word can function as a loving and compassionate mother or father to you. You can learn from the Scriptures and then create a legacy of wisdom as you teach your own children.

• **4:5–7** If you want wisdom, you must decide to go after it. It takes resolve—a determination not to abandon the search once you begin no matter how difficult the road may become. This is not a once-in-a-lifetime step, but a daily process of choosing between two paths—the wicked (4:14–17, 19) and the righteous (4:18). Nothing else is more important or more valuable.

4:7 David taught Solomon as a young boy that seeking God's wisdom was the most important choice he could make. Solomon learned the lesson well. When God appeared to the new king to fulfill any request, Solomon chose wisdom above all else. We should also make God's wisdom our first choice. We don't have to wait for God to appear to us. We can boldly ask him for wisdom today through prayer. James 1:5 assures us that God will grant our request.

4:7 Ps 119:104 Prov 23:23

[7]Wisdom is supreme; therefore get wisdom.
Though it cost all you have,[a] get understanding.
[8]Esteem her, and she will exalt you;
embrace her, and she will honor you.
[9]She will set a garland of grace on your head
and present you with a crown of splendor."

[10]Listen, my son, accept what I say,
and the years of your life will be many.
[11]I guide you in the way of wisdom
and lead you along straight paths.

4:12 Ps 37:23; 91:11

[12]When you walk, your steps will not be hampered;
when you run, you will not stumble.

4:13 Jn 6:63

[13]Hold on to instruction, do not let it go;
guard it well, for it is your life.

4:14 Ps 1:1

[14]Do not set foot on the path of the wicked
or walk in the way of evil men.
[15]Avoid it, do not travel on it;
turn from it and go on your way.

4:16 Ps 36:4 Mic 2:1

[16]For they cannot sleep till they do evil;
they are robbed of slumber till they make someone fall.
[17]They eat the bread of wickedness
and drink the wine of violence.

[18]The path of the righteous is like the first gleam of dawn,
shining ever brighter till the full light of day.

4:19 Jn 1:4,5

[19]But the way of the wicked is like deep darkness;
they do not know what makes them stumble.

[20]My son, pay attention to what I say;
listen closely to my words.
[21]Do not let them out of your sight,
keep them within your heart;
[22]for they are life to those who find them
and health to a man's whole body.

4:23 Lk 6:45

[23]Above all else, guard your heart,
for it is the wellspring of life.

[a] 7 Or *Whatever else you get*

STRATEGY FOR EFFECTIVE LIVING			
	Begins with	God's Wisdom	Respecting and appreciating who God is. Reverence and awe in recognizing the almighty God.
	Requires	Moral Application	Trusting in God and his Word. Allowing his Word to speak to us personally. Willing to obey.
	Requires	Practical Application	Acting on God's direction in daily devotions.
	Results in	Effective Living	Experiencing what God does with our obedience.

4:16, 17 It is difficult for people to accept the fact that friends and aquaintances might be luring them to do wrong. Young people want to be accepted, so they would never want to confront or criticize a friend for wrong plans or actions. Many other people can't even see how their friends' actions could lead to trouble. While we should be accepting of others, we need a healthy scepticism about human behavior. When you feel yourself being heavily influenced, proceed with caution. Don't let your friends cause you to fall into sin.

4:23–27 Our heart—our feelings of love and desire—dictates to a great extent how we live, because we always find time to do what we enjoy. Solomon tells us to guard our heart above all else, making sure we concentrate on those desires that will keep us on the right path. Make sure your affections push you in the right direction. Put boundaries on your desires: don't go after everything you see. Look straight ahead, keep your eyes fixed on your goal, and don't get sidetracked on detours that lead to sin.

[24]Put away perversity from your mouth;
keep corrupt talk far from your lips.
[25]Let your eyes look straight ahead,
fix your gaze directly before you.
[26]Make level[a] paths for your feet
and take only ways that are firm.
[27]Do not swerve to the right or the left;
keep your foot from evil.

4:25 Job 31:1 Mt 6:22
4:26 Prov 5:21 Heb 12:13
4:27 Deut 5:32; 28:14

Warning Against Adultery

5

My son, pay attention to my wisdom,
listen well to my words of insight,
[2]that you may maintain discretion
and your lips may preserve knowledge.
[3]For the lips of an adulteress drip honey,
and her speech is smoother than oil;
[4]but in the end she is bitter as gall,
sharp as a double-edged sword.
[5]Her feet go down to death;
her steps lead straight to the grave.[b]
[6]She gives no thought to the way of life;
her paths are crooked, but she knows it not.

[7]Now then, my sons, listen to me;
do not turn aside from what I say.
[8]Keep to a path far from her,
do not go near the door of her house,
[9]lest you give your best strength to others
and your years to one who is cruel,
[10]lest strangers feast on your wealth
and your toil enrich another man's house.
[11]At the end of your life you will groan,
when your flesh and body are spent.
[12]You will say, "How I hated discipline!
How my heart spurned correction!
[13]I would not obey my teachers
or listen to my instructors.
[14]I have come to the brink of utter ruin
in the midst of the whole assembly."

5:3 Ps 55:21 Prov 5:20; 7:5
5:4 Eccles 7:26
5:8 Prov 7:25; 9:14 2 Tim 2:22
5:11 Prov 3:35
5:13 Lk 15:18

[a] 26 Or *Consider the* [b] 5 Hebrew *Sheol*

- **5:3** This *adulteress* is a prostitute. Proverbs includes many warnings against illicit sex for several reasons. First, a prostitute's charm is used as an example of any temptation to do wrong or to leave the pursuit of wisdom. Second, sexual immorality of any kind was and still is extremely dangerous. It destroys family life. It erodes a person's ability to love. It degrades human beings and turns them into objects. It can lead to disease. It can result in unwanted children. Third, sexual immorality is against God's law.
- **5:3–8** Any person should be on guard against those who use flattery and smooth speech (lips that "drip honey") that would lead him or her into sin. The best advice is to take a detour and avoid even conversation with such people.
- **5:11–13** At the end of your life, it will be too late to ask for advice. When desire is fully activated, people don't want advice—they want satisfaction. The best time to learn the dangers and foolishness of going after forbidden sex (or anything else that is harmful) is long before the temptation comes. Resistance is easier if the decision has already been made. Don't wait to see what happens. Prepare for temptation by deciding *now* how you will act when you face it.
- **5:15** "Drink water from your own cistern" is a picture of faithfulness in marriage. In desert lands, water is precious, and a well is a family's most important possession. In Old Testament times, it was considered a crime to steal water from someone else's well, just as it was a crime to have intercourse with another man's wife. In both cases, the offender is endangering the health and security of family.
- **5:15–21** In contrast to much of what we read, see, and hear today, this passage urges couples to look to each other for lifelong satisfaction and companionship. Many temptations entice husbands and wives to desert each other for excitement and pleasures to be found elsewhere, when marriage becomes dull. But God designed marriage and sanctified it, and only within this covenant relationship can we find real love and fulfillment. Don't let God's best for you be wasted on the illusion of greener pastures elsewhere. Instead, rejoice with your spouse as you give yourselves to God and to each other.

5:15 Eccles 9:9 Song 4:15

[15]Drink water from your own cistern,
running water from your own well.
[16]Should your springs overflow in the streets,
your streams of water in the public squares?
[17]Let them be yours alone,
never to be shared with strangers.

5:18 Eccles 9:9 Mal 2:14

[18]May your fountain be blessed,
and may you rejoice in the wife of your youth.

5:19 Song 4:5; 7:3

[19]A loving doe, a graceful deer—
may her breasts satisfy you always,
may you ever be captivated by her love.
[20]Why be captivated, my son, by an adulteress?
Why embrace the bosom of another man's wife?

5:21 Job 14:16

[21]For a man's ways are in full view of the LORD,
and he examines all his paths.

5:22 Num 32:23

[22]The evil deeds of a wicked man ensnare him;
the cords of his sin hold him fast.
[23]He will die for lack of discipline,
led astray by his own great folly.

Warnings Against Folly

6:1 Prov 17:18 22:26; 27:13

6 My son, if you have put up security for your neighbor,
if you have struck hands in pledge for another,
[2]if you have been trapped by what you said,
ensnared by the words of your mouth,
[3]then do this, my son, to free yourself,
since you have fallen into your neighbor's hands:
Go and humble yourself;
press your plea with your neighbor!
[4]Allow no sleep to your eyes,
no slumber to your eyelids.
[5]Free yourself, like a gazelle from the hand of the hunter,
like a bird from the snare of the fowler.

THINGS GOD HATES
The book of Proverbs notes 14 types of people and actions that God hates. Let these be guidelines of what we are *not* to be and do!

Violent people	Proverbs 3:31
Haughtiness, lying, murdering, scheming, eagerness to do evil, a false witness, stirring up dissension	Proverbs 6:16–19
Those who are untruthful	Proverbs 12:22
The sacrifice of the wicked	Proverbs 15:8
The way of the wicked	Proverbs 15:9
The thoughts of the wicked	Proverbs 15:26
Those who are proud	Proverbs 16:5
Those who judge unjustly	Proverbs 17:15

• **5:18–20** God does not intend faithfulness in marriage to be boring, lifeless, pleasureless, and dull. Sex is a gift God gives to married people for their mutual enjoyment. Real happiness comes when we decide to find pleasure in the relationship God has given or will give us, and to commit ourselves to making it pleasurable for our spouse. The real danger is in doubting that God knows and cares for us. We then may resent his timing and carelessly pursue sexual pleasure without his blessing.

6:1–5 These verses are not against generosity, but against overextending one's financial resources and acting in irresponsible ways that could lead to poverty. It is important to maintain a balance between generosity and good stewardship. God wants us to help our friends and the needy, but he does not promise to cover the costs of every unwise commitment we make. We should also act responsibly so that our family does not suffer.

6:6–11 Proverbs warns against giving in to the temptation of laziness, of sleeping instead of working. This does not mean we should never rest: God gave the Jews the Sabbath, a weekly day of rest and restoration. But we should not rest when we should be working. The ant is used as an example because it utilizes its energy and resources economically. If laziness turns us from our responsibilities, poverty will soon bar us from the legitimate rest we should enjoy. (See also the chart in chapter 28.)

[6]Go to the ant, you sluggard;
consider its ways and be wise!
[7]It has no commander,
no overseer or ruler,
[8]yet it stores its provisions in summer
and gathers its food at harvest.

[9]How long will you lie there, you sluggard?
When will you get up from your sleep?
[10]A little sleep, a little slumber,
a little folding of the hands to rest—
[11]and poverty will come on you like a bandit
and scarcity like an armed man.[a]

[12]A scoundrel and villain,
who goes about with a corrupt mouth,
[13] who winks with his eye,
signals with his feet
and motions with his fingers,
[14] who plots evil with deceit in his heart—
he always stirs up dissension.
[15]Therefore disaster will overtake him in an instant;
he will suddenly be destroyed—without remedy.

[16]There are six things the LORD hates,
seven that are detestable to him:
[17] haughty eyes,
a lying tongue,
hands that shed innocent blood,
[18] a heart that devises wicked schemes,
feet that are quick to rush into evil,
[19] a false witness who pours out lies
and a man who stirs up dissension among brothers.

6:6 Prov 10:26 13:4; 30:24,25

6:10 Prov 24:33,34

6:11 Prov 24:34

6:12 Prov 8:13; 16:27

6:14 Prov 10:32 17:11

6:16-19 Gen 6:5 Prov 1:16; 6:14 19:5,9; 21:4 24:2; 28:17 30:21 Isa 1:15

Warning Against Adultery

[20]My son, keep your father's commands
and do not forsake your mother's teaching.
[21]Bind them upon your heart forever;
fasten them around your neck.
[22]When you walk, they will guide you;
when you sleep, they will watch over you;
when you awake, they will speak to you.
[23]For these commands are a lamp,
this teaching is a light,
and the corrections of discipline
are the way to life,
[24]keeping you from the immoral woman,
from the smooth tongue of the wayward wife.

6:23 Ps 119:105 Prov 13:9

[a] 11 Or *like a vagrant / and scarcity like a beggar*

6:20–23 It is natural and good for children, as they grow toward adulthood, to become increasingly independent of their parents. Young adults, however, should take care not to turn a deaf ear to their parents—to reject their advice just when it is needed most. If you are struggling with a decision or looking for insight, check with your parents or other older adults who know you well. Their extra years of experience may have given them the wisdom you seek.

• **6:25** Regard lust as a warning sign of danger ahead. When you notice that you are attracted to a person of the opposite sex or preoccupied with thoughts of him or her, your desires may lead you to sin. Ask God to help you change your desires before you are drawn into sin.

• **6:25–35** Some people argue that it is all right to break God's law against sexual sin if nobody gets hurt. In truth, somebody always gets hurt. Spouses are devastated. Children are scarred. The partners themselves, even if they escape disease and unwanted pregnancy, lose their ability to fulfill commitments, to feel sexual desire, to trust, and to be entirely open with another person. God's laws are not arbitrary. They do not forbid good, clean fun; rather, they warn us against destroying ourselves through unwise actions.

6:25 2 Kgs 9:30 Prov 21:4 Mt 5:28

[25]Do not lust in your heart after her beauty
or let her captivate you with her eyes,
[26]for the prostitute reduces you to a loaf of bread,
and the adulteress preys upon your very life.
[27]Can a man scoop fire into his lap
without his clothes being burned?
[28]Can a man walk on hot coals
without his feet being scorched?

6:29 Prov 16:5 Jer 5:8 Ezek 22:11

[29]So is he who sleeps with another man's wife;
no one who touches her will go unpunished.

[30]Men do not despise a thief if he steals
to satisfy his hunger when he is starving.

6:31 Ex 22:7

[31]Yet if he is caught, he must pay sevenfold,
though it costs him all the wealth of his house.

6:32 Prov 7:7,22,23 9:14,16

[32]But a man who commits adultery lacks judgment;
whoever does so destroys himself.

6:33 Ps 51:8 Prov 18:3

[33]Blows and disgrace are his lot,
and his shame will never be wiped away;

6:34 Lev 20:10 Prov 27:4 Song 8:6

[34]for jealousy arouses a husband's fury,
and he will show no mercy when he takes revenge.
[35]He will not accept any compensation;
he will refuse the bribe, however great it is.

Warning Against the Adulteress

7 My son, keep my words
and store up my commands within you.

7:2 Ps 17:8 Prov 4:4; 9:11 10:27; 16:22

[2]Keep my commands and you will live;
guard my teachings as the apple of your eye.

7:3 Deut 6:8

[3]Bind them on your fingers;
write them on the tablet of your heart.
[4]Say to wisdom, "You are my sister,"
and call understanding your kinsman;

7:5 Prov 4:24; 22:14

[5]they will keep you from the adulteress,
from the wayward wife with her seductive words.

[6]At the window of my house
I looked out through the lattice.

7:7 Prov 1:22; 6:32 8:5; 22:3

[7]I saw among the simple,
I noticed among the young men,
a youth who lacked judgment.

7:8 Prov 4:14,15 5:8; 7:12,27

[8]He was going down the street near her corner,
walking along in the direction of her house
[9]at twilight, as the day was fading,
as the dark of night set in.

7:10 Gen 38:14,15 Isa 3:16; 23:16

[10]Then out came a woman to meet him,
dressed like a prostitute and with crafty intent.

7:11 Prov 9:13; 23:28

[11](She is loud and defiant,
her feet never stay at home;
[12]now in the street, now in the squares,
at every corner she lurks.)

• **7:6–23** Although this advice is directed toward young men, young women should heed it as well. The person who has no purpose in life is simple (7:7). Without aim or direction, an empty life is unstable, vulnerable to many temptations. Even though the young man in this passage doesn't know where he is going, the adulteress knows where she wants him. Notice her strategies: she is dressed to allure men (7:10); her approach is bold (7:13); she invites him over to her place (7:16–18); she cunningly answers his every objection (7:19, 20); she persuades him with smooth talk (7:21); she traps him (7:23). To combat temptation, make sure your life is full of God's Word and wisdom (7:4). Recognize the strategies of temptation, and run away from them—fast.

[13]She took hold of him and kissed him
and with a brazen face she said:

[14]"I have fellowship offerings[a] at home;
today I fulfilled my vows.
[15]So I came out to meet you;
I looked for you and have found you!
[16]I have covered my bed
with colored linens from Egypt.
[17]I have perfumed my bed
with myrrh, aloes and cinnamon.
[18]Come, let's drink deep of love till morning;
let's enjoy ourselves with love!
[19]My husband is not at home;
he has gone on a long journey.
[20]He took his purse filled with money
and will not be home till full moon."

[21]With persuasive words she led him astray;
she seduced him with her smooth talk.
[22]All at once he followed her
like an ox going to the slaughter,
like a deer[b] stepping into a noose[c]
[23] till an arrow pierces his liver,
like a bird darting into a snare,
little knowing it will cost him his life.

[24]Now then, my sons, listen to me;
pay attention to what I say.
[25]Do not let your heart turn to her ways
or stray into her paths.
[26]Many are the victims she has brought down;
her slain are a mighty throng.
[27]Her house is a highway to the grave,[d]
leading down to the chambers of death.

Wisdom's Call

8 Does not wisdom call out?
Does not understanding raise her voice?
[2]On the heights along the way,
where the paths meet, she takes her stand;
[3]beside the gates leading into the city,
at the entrances, she cries aloud:
[4]"To you, O men, I call out;
I raise my voice to all mankind.
[5]You who are simple, gain prudence;
you who are foolish, gain understanding.
[6]Listen, for I have worthy things to say;
I open my lips to speak what is right.

7:16 Prov 31:22; Ezek 27:7
7:21 Prov 5:3; 6:24
7:23 Prov 1:17; Eccles 9:12
7:24 Prov 4:1; 5:7
7:25 Prov 4:23; 5:8
7:27 Prov 2:18; 5:5
8:1 Job 19:7

[a] *14* Traditionally *peace offerings* [b] *22* Syriac (see also Septuagint); Hebrew *fool* [c] *22* The meaning of the Hebrew for this line is uncertain. [d] *27* Hebrew *Sheol*

• **7:25–27** There are definite steps you can take to avoid sexual sins. First, guard your mind. Don't read books, look at pictures, or encourage fantasies that stimulate the wrong desires. Second, keep away from settings and friends that tempt you to sin. Third, don't think only of the moment—focus on the future. Today's thrill may lead to tomorrow's ruin.

• **8:1ff** Wisdom's call is contrasted to the call of the adulteress in chapter 7. Wisdom is portrayed as a woman who guides us (8:1–13) and makes us succeed (8:14–21). Wisdom was present at the creation and works with the Creator (8:22–31). God approves of those who listen to wisdom's counsel (8:32–35). Those who hate wisdom love death (8:36). Wisdom should affect every aspect of our entire lives, from beginning to end. Be sure to open all corners of your life to God's direction and guidance.

[7]My mouth speaks what is true,
for my lips detest wickedness.
[8]All the words of my mouth are just;
none of them is crooked or perverse.
[9]To the discerning all of them are right;
they are faultless to those who have knowledge.
[10]Choose my instruction instead of silver,
knowledge rather than choice gold,
[11]for wisdom is more precious than rubies,
and nothing you desire can compare with her.

[12]"I, wisdom, dwell together with prudence;
I possess knowledge and discretion.
[13]To fear the LORD is to hate evil;
I hate pride and arrogance,
evil behavior and perverse speech.
[14]Counsel and sound judgment are mine;
I have understanding and power.
[15]By me kings reign
and rulers make laws that are just;
[16]by me princes govern,
and all nobles who rule on earth.[a]
[17]I love those who love me,
and those who seek me find me.
[18]With me are riches and honor,
enduring wealth and prosperity.
[19]My fruit is better than fine gold;
what I yield surpasses choice silver.
[20]I walk in the way of righteousness,
along the paths of justice,
[21]bestowing wealth on those who love me
and making their treasuries full.

[22]"The LORD brought me forth as the first of his works,[b,c]
before his deeds of old;
[23]I was appointed[d] from eternity,
from the beginning, before the world began.
[24]When there were no oceans, I was given birth,
when there were no springs abounding with water;
[25]before the mountains were settled in place,
before the hills, I was given birth,
[26]before he made the earth or its fields
or any of the dust of the world.
[27]I was there when he set the heavens in place,
when he marked out the horizon on the face of the deep,
[28]when he established the clouds above
and fixed securely the fountains of the deep,
[29]when he gave the sea its boundary
so the waters would not overstep his command,
and when he marked out the foundations of the earth.

8:10 Ps 119:72,127
8:11 Prov 3:14,15; 16:16; 20:15
8:13 Isa 13:11
8:14 Isa 1:26; Rom 13:1
8:17 1 Sam 2:30; Jn 14:21
8:18 Ps 112:3; Mt 6:33
8:20 Ps 23:3; 25:4; Isa 2:3
8:22 Job 28:27; Ps 104:24
8:23 Jn 17:5,24
8:24 Gen 1:9; Job 38:16
8:27 Job 26:10; 38:6; Ps 33:6; 104:5

[a] 16 Many Hebrew manuscripts and Septuagint; most Hebrew manuscripts *and nobles—all righteous rulers*
[b] 22 Or *way*; or *dominion* [c] 22 Or *The LORD possessed me at the beginning of his work*; or *The LORD brought me forth at the beginning of his work* [d] 23 Or *fashioned*

8:13 The more a person fears and respects God, the more he or she will hate evil. Love for God and love for sin cannot coexist. Harboring secret sins means that you are tolerating evil within yourself. Make a clean break with sin and commit yourself completely to God.

8:22–31 God says wisdom is primary and fundamental. It is the foundation on which all life is built. Paul and John may have alluded to some of Solomon's statements about wisdom to describe Christ's presence at the creation of the world (Colossians 1:15–17; 2:2, 3; Revelation 3:14).

[30] Then I was the craftsman at his side.
I was filled with delight day after day,
rejoicing always in his presence,
[31]rejoicing in his whole world
and delighting in mankind.

[32]"Now then, my sons, listen to me;
blessed are those who keep my ways.
[33]Listen to my instruction and be wise;
do not ignore it.
[34]Blessed is the man who listens to me,
watching daily at my doors,
waiting at my doorway.
[35]For whoever finds me finds life
and receives favor from the LORD.
[36]But whoever fails to find me harms himself;
all who hate me love death."

8:32 Prov 5:7; 29:18
8:34 Ps 27:4 Prov 1:21
8:35 Jn 17:3
8:36 Prov 15:32

Invitations of Wisdom and of Folly

9 Wisdom has built her house;
she has hewn out its seven pillars.
[2]She has prepared her meat and mixed her wine;
she has also set her table.
[3]She has sent out her maids, and she calls
from the highest point of the city.
[4]"Let all who are simple come in here!"
she says to those who lack judgment.
[5]"Come, eat my food
and drink the wine I have mixed.
[6]Leave your simple ways and you will live;
walk in the way of understanding.

[7]"Whoever corrects a mocker invites insult;
whoever rebukes a wicked man incurs abuse.
[8]Do not rebuke a mocker or he will hate you;
rebuke a wise man and he will love you.
[9]Instruct a wise man and he will be wiser still;
teach a righteous man and he will add to his learning.

[10]"The fear of the LORD is the beginning of wisdom,
and knowledge of the Holy One is understanding.
[11]For through me your days will be many,
and years will be added to your life.
[12]If you are wise, your wisdom will reward you;
if you are a mocker, you alone will suffer."

9:1 Eph 2:20 Heb 3:5,6 1 Pet 2:5
9:3 Mt 22:3
9:6 Prov 3:22; 4:22 9:11; 16:22
9:9 Prov 1:5; 25:12
9:10 Job 28:28 Ps 111:10
9:12 Job 22:2 Gal 6:5

9:1 The seven pillars are figurative; they do not represent seven principles of wisdom. In the Bible, the number seven represents completeness and perfection. This verse poetically states that wisdom lacks nothing – it is complete and perfect.

• **9:1ff** Wisdom and Folly (foolishness) are portrayed in this chapter as rival young women, each preparing a feast and inviting people to it. But Wisdom is a responsible woman of character, while Folly is a prostitute serving stolen food. Wisdom appeals first to the mind; Folly to the senses. It is easier to excite the senses, but the pleasures of Folly are temporary. By contrast, the satisfaction that wisdom brings lasts forever.

9:1–5 The banquet described in this chapter has some interesting parallels to the banquet Jesus described in one of his parables (Luke 14:15–24). Many may intend to go, but they never make it because they get sidetracked by other activities that seem more important at the time. Don't let anything become more important than your search for God's wisdom.

• **9:7–10** Are you a mocker or a wise person? You can tell by the way you respond to criticism. Instead of tossing back a quick put-down or clever retort when rebuked, listen to what is being said. Learn from your critics; this is the path to wisdom. Wisdom begins with knowing God. He gives insight into living because he created life. To know God is not just to know the facts about him, but to stand in awe of him and have a relationship with him. Do you really want to be wise? Get to know God better and better. (See James 1:5, 2 Peter 1:2–4 for more on how to become wise.)

[13]The woman Folly is loud;
she is undisciplined and without knowledge.
[14]She sits at the door of her house,
on a seat at the highest point of the city,
[15]calling out to those who pass by,
who go straight on their way.
[16]"Let all who are simple come in here!"
she says to those who lack judgment.
[17]"Stolen water is sweet;
food eaten in secret is delicious!"
[18]But little do they know that the dead are there,
that her guests are in the depths of the grave.[a]

9:17 Prov 20:17 30:20

B. WISDOM FOR ALL PEOPLE (10:1–24:34)

These short couplets are what we commonly recognize as proverbs. They cover a wide range of topics. The first section was written by Solomon. The next two sections were written by others, but collected by Solomon. These sayings give people practical wisdom for godly living at every stage of life.

Proverbs of Solomon

10 The proverbs of Solomon:

A wise son brings joy to his father,
but a foolish son grief to his mother.

[2]Ill-gotten treasures are of no value,
but righteousness delivers from death.

[3]The LORD does not let the righteous go hungry
but he thwarts the craving of the wicked.

[4]Lazy hands make a man poor,
but diligent hands bring wealth.

[5]He who gathers crops in summer is a wise son,
but he who sleeps during harvest is a disgraceful son.

[6]Blessings crown the head of the righteous,
but violence overwhelms the mouth of the wicked.[b]

[7]The memory of the righteous will be a blessing,
but the name of the wicked will rot.

[8]The wise in heart accept commands,
but a chattering fool comes to ruin.

10:1 Prov 15:20
10:3 Ps 34:9,10 37:25 Mt 6:33
10:4 Prov 6:6
10:6 Prov 28:20
10:7 Ps 9:5,6 109:13; 112:6
10:8 Mt 7:24

[a] *18* Hebrew *Sheol* [b] *6* Or *but the mouth of the wicked conceals violence*; also in verse 11

• **9:14–17** There is something hypnotic and intoxicating about wickedness. One sin leads us to want more; sinful behavior seems more exciting than the Christian life. That is why many people put aside all thought of wisdom's sumptuous banquet (9:1–5) in order to eat the stolen food of Folly. Don't be deceived—sin is dangerous. Before reaching for forbidden fruit, take a long look at what happens to those who eat it. (See the chart in chapter 21.)

10:2 Some people bring unhappiness on themselves by choosing ill-gotten treasures. For example, craving satisfaction, they may do something that destroys their chances of ever achieving happiness. God's principles for right living bring lasting happiness because they guide us into long-term right behavior in spite of our ever-changing feelings.

10:3 Proverbs is full of verses contrasting the righteous person with the wicked. These statements are not intended to apply universally to all people in every situation. For example, some good people do go hungry. Rather, they are intended to communicate the general truth that the life of the person who seeks God is better in the long run than the life of the wicked person, which leads to ruin. These statements are not ironclad promises, but general truths. In addition, God desires a just government that cares for the poor and needy—the kind of government Israel was intended to have (see Deuteronomy 24:17–22). A corrupt government often thwarts the plans of good men and women.

• **10:4, 5** Every day has 24 hours filled with opportunities to grow, serve, and be productive. Yet it is so easy to waste time, letting life slip from our grasp. Refuse to be a lazy person, sleeping or frittering away the hours meant for productive work. See time as God's gift and seize your opportunities to live diligently for him.

[9]The man of integrity walks securely,
but he who takes crooked paths will be found out.

[10]He who winks maliciously causes grief,
and a chattering fool comes to ruin.

[11]The mouth of the righteous is a fountain of life,
but violence overwhelms the mouth of the wicked.

[12]Hatred stirs up dissension,
but love covers over all wrongs.

[13]Wisdom is found on the lips of the discerning,
but a rod is for the back of him who lacks judgment.

[14]Wise men store up knowledge,
but the mouth of a fool invites ruin.

[15]The wealth of the rich is their fortified city,
but poverty is the ruin of the poor.

[16]The wages of the righteous bring them life,
but the income of the wicked brings them punishment.

[17]He who heeds discipline shows the way to life,
but whoever ignores correction leads others astray.

[18]He who conceals his hatred has lying lips,
and whoever spreads slander is a fool.

[19]When words are many, sin is not absent,
but he who holds his tongue is wise.

[20]The tongue of the righteous is choice silver,
but the heart of the wicked is of little value.

[21]The lips of the righteous nourish many,
but fools die for lack of judgment.

[22]The blessing of the LORD brings wealth,
and he adds no trouble to it.

[23]A fool finds pleasure in evil conduct,
but a man of understanding delights in wisdom.

[24]What the wicked dreads will overtake him;
what the righteous desire will be granted.

[25]When the storm has swept by, the wicked are gone,
but the righteous stand firm forever.

10:9 Ps 23:4; Prov 3:23; 26:27; Isa 33:15,16; Mt 10:26
10:10 Prov 6:13
10:11 Ps 37:20; Prov 13:14; 18:4
10:12 Prov 17:9; 1 Cor 13:4-7
10:14 Prov 13:3; 18:7; Jas 3:2,5
10:15 Prov 18:11; 19:7
10:17 Prov 6:23; 12:1; 22:17
10:18 Prov 26:24
10:19 Job 11:2; Prov 18:21
10:21 Prov 12:18; 15:4; Hos 4:6
10:22 Gen 24:35; 26:12; Deut 8:18
10:23 Prov 2:14; 15:21
10:24 Job 15:21; Prov 1:27; 15:8
10:25 Ps 15:1-5; 125:1

10:9, 10 Sin is serious not just because of what it does to us and to others, but because it is personal rebellion against God. He does not take sin lightly, and we dare not either. If there is an area in your life that you have been withholding from God's control, end your rebellion. If you have minimized and rationalized disobedience, put aside your excuses. Don't wink at sin. Boldly confront it and confess it to God, because sin is serious business.

• **10:18** By hating another person you may become a liar or a fool. If you try to conceal your hate, you end up lying. If you slander the other person and are proven wrong, you are a fool. The only way out is to admit your hateful feelings to God. Ask him to change your heart, to help you love instead of hate.

10:20 A lot of poor advice is worth less than a little good advice. It is easy to get opinions from people who will tell us only what they think will please us, but such advice is not helpful. Instead we should look for those who will speak the truth, even when it hurts. Think about the people to whom you go for advice. What do you expect to hear from them?

10:22 God supplies most people with the personal and financial abilities to respond to the needs of others. If we all realized how God has blessed us, and if we all used our resources to do God's will, hunger and poverty would be wiped out. Wealth is a blessing only if we use it in the way God intended.

10:24 The wicked person dreads death. Those who do not believe in God usually fear death, and with good reason. By contrast, believers desire eternal life and God's salvation—their hopes will be rewarded. This verse offers a choice: you can have either your fears or your desires come true. You make that choice by rejecting God and living your own way, or by accepting God and following him.

10:27 Ps 55:23 Prov 14:27
10:28 Job 11:20
10:30 Ps 37:25; 125:1 Prov 2:22
10:31 Ps 37:30
10:32 Prov 6:12 Eccles 12:10
11:1 Deut 25:13-16
11:2 Prov 16:18
11:3 Prov 13:6; 21:7 22:12
11:4 Ezek 7:19 1 Tim 4:8; 6:7
11:6 Ps 7:15,16 9:15
11:8 Ps 22:8 51:14,15

26As vinegar to the teeth and smoke to the eyes,
so is a sluggard to those who send him.

27The fear of the LORD adds length to life,
but the years of the wicked are cut short.

28The prospect of the righteous is joy,
but the hopes of the wicked come to nothing.

29The way of the LORD is a refuge for the righteous,
but it is the ruin of those who do evil.

30The righteous will never be uprooted,
but the wicked will not remain in the land.

31The mouth of the righteous brings forth wisdom,
but a perverse tongue will be cut out.

32The lips of the righteous know what is fitting,
but the mouth of the wicked only what is perverse.

11 The LORD abhors dishonest scales,
but accurate weights are his delight.

2When pride comes, then comes disgrace,
but with humility comes wisdom.

3The integrity of the upright guides them,
but the unfaithful are destroyed by their duplicity.

4Wealth is worthless in the day of wrath,
but righteousness delivers from death.

5The righteousness of the blameless makes a straight way for them,
but the wicked are brought down by their own wickedness.

6The righteousness of the upright delivers them,
but the unfaithful are trapped by evil desires.

7When a wicked man dies, his hope perishes;
all he expected from his power comes to nothing.

8The righteous man is rescued from trouble,
and it comes on the wicked instead.

GOD'S ADVICE ABOUT MONEY

Proverbs gives some practical instruction on the use of money, although sometimes it is advice we would rather not hear. It's more comfortable to continue in our habits than to learn how to use money more wisely. The advice includes:

Be generous in giving	11:24, 25; 22:9
Place people's needs ahead of profit	11:26
Be cautious of countersigning for another	17:18; 22:26, 27
Don't accept bribes	17:23
Help the poor	19:17; 21:13
Store up for the future	21:20
Be careful about borrowing	22:7

Other verses to study include: 11:15; 20:16; 25:14; 27:13

11:4 "The day of wrath" refers to the time of our death or to the time when God settles accounts with all people. On judgment day, each of us will stand alone, accountable for all our deeds. At that time, no amount of riches will buy reconciliation with God. Only our love for and obedience to God will count.

11:7, 8 These verses, like 10:3, contrasts two paths in life, but is not intended to apply universally to all people in all circumstances. It does not exclude God's people from problems or struggles. If a person follows God's wisdom, however, God can rescue him from trouble. But a wicked person will fall into his or her own traps. Even if a good person suffers, he can be sure he will ultimately be rescued from eternal death.

[9]With his mouth the godless destroys his neighbor,
but through knowledge the righteous escape.

[10]When the righteous prosper, the city rejoices;
when the wicked perish, there are shouts of joy.

11:10 Prov 28:28

[11]Through the blessing of the upright a city is exalted,
but by the mouth of the wicked it is destroyed.

[12]A man who lacks judgment derides his neighbor,
but a man of understanding holds his tongue.

11:12 Prov 10:14 13:3; 18:7

[13]A gossip betrays a confidence,
but a trustworthy man keeps a secret.

11:13 Prov 19:11 20:19 1 Tim 5:13

[14]For lack of guidance a nation falls,
but many advisers make victory sure.

11:14 Prov 15:22 20:18; 24:6

[15]He who puts up security for another will surely suffer,
but whoever refuses to strike hands in pledge is safe.

11:15 Prov 6:1; 27:13

[16]A kindhearted woman gains respect,
but ruthless men gain only wealth.

[17]A kind man benefits himself,
but a cruel man brings trouble on himself.

11:17 Mt 5:7; 25:34-36

[18]The wicked man earns deceptive wages,
but he who sows righteousness reaps a sure reward.

11:18 Hos 10:12

[19]The truly righteous man attains life,
but he who pursues evil goes to his death.

11:19 Prov 10:16 19:23; 21:16 Rom 6:23

[20]The LORD detests men of perverse heart
but he delights in those whose ways are blameless.

11:20 Ps 75:5

[21]Be sure of this: The wicked will not go unpunished,
but those who are righteous will go free.

[22]Like a gold ring in a pig's snout
is a beautiful woman who shows no discretion.

11:22 Ezek 16:15 1 Pet 3:3

[23]The desire of the righteous ends only in good,
but the hope of the wicked only in wrath.

11:23 Rom 2:8,9

[24]One man gives freely, yet gains even more;
another withholds unduly, but comes to poverty.

11:24 Prov 3:9,10 Mt 5:7 2 Cor 9:6,7

• **11:9** The mouth can be used either as a weapon or a tool, hurting relationships or building them up. Sadly, it is often easier to destroy than to build, and most people have received more destructive comments than those that build up. Every person you meet today is either a demolition site or a construction opportunity. Your words will make a difference. Will they be weapons for destruction or tools for construction?

11:14 A good leader needs and uses wise advisers. One person's perspective and understanding is severely limited; he or she may not have all the facts or may be blinded by bias, emotions, or wrong impressions. To be a wise leader at home, at church, or at work, seek the counsel of others and be open to their advice. Then, after considering all the facts, make your decision. (See the chart in chapter 30.)

• **11:19** A righteous person attains life because he or she lives life more fully each day. He also attains life because people usually live longer when they live right, with proper diet, exercise, and rest. In addition, he need not fear death because eternal life is God's gift to him (John 11:25). By contrast, the evil person not only finds eternal death, but also misses out on real life on earth.

• **11:22** Physical attractiveness without discretion soon wears thin. We are to seek those character strengths that help us make wise decisions, not just those that make us look good. Not everyone who looks good is pleasant to live or work with. While taking good care of our body and appearance is not wrong, we also need to develop our ability to think.

11:24, 25 These two verses present a paradox: that we become richer by being generous. The world says to hold on to as much as possible, but God blesses those who give freely of their possessions, time, and energy. When we give, God supplies us with more so that we can give more. In addition, giving helps us gain a right perspective on our possessions. We realize they were never really

25A generous man will prosper;
he who refreshes others will himself be refreshed.

11:26 Gen 41:56,57 Amos 8:4

26People curse the man who hoards grain,
but blessing crowns him who is willing to sell.

11:27 Prov 17:11

27He who seeks good finds goodwill,
but evil comes to him who searches for it.

11:28 Ps 1:2,3; 92:12 Jer 17:7,8 Mk 10:24,25 1 Tim 6:17

28Whoever trusts in his riches will fall,
but the righteous will thrive like a green leaf.

11:29 Prov 14:19 15:27

29He who brings trouble on his family will inherit only wind,
and the fool will be servant to the wise.

11:30 Jas 5:20

30The fruit of the righteous is a tree of life,
and he who wins souls is wise.

31If the righteous receive their due on earth,
how much more the ungodly and the sinner!

12:1 Prov 25:12

12 Whoever loves discipline loves knowledge,
but he who hates correction is stupid.

2A good man obtains favor from the LORD,
but the LORD condemns a crafty man.

TEACHING AND LEARNING

Good teaching comes from good learning—and Proverbs has more to say to students than to teachers. Proverbs is concerned with the learning of wisdom. The book makes it clear that there are no good alternatives to learning wisdom. We are either becoming wise learners or refusing to learn and becoming foolish failures. Proverbs encourages us to make the right choice.

Wise Learners	*Proverb(s)*	*Foolish Failures*
Quietly accept instruction and criticism	10:8; 23:12; 25:12	Ignore instruction
Love discipline	12:1	Hate correction
Listen to advice	12:15; 21:11; 24:6	Think they need no advice
Accept parents' discipline	13:1	Mock parents
Lead others to life	10:17	Lead others astray
Receive honor	13:18	End in poverty and shame
Profit from constructive rebuke	15:31, 32; 29:1	Self-destruct by refusing rebuke

Advice to teachers:
Help people avoid traps (13:14).
Use pleasant words (16:21).
Speak at the right time (15:23; 18:20).

ours to begin with, but were given to us by God to be used to help others. What then do we gain by giving? Freedom from enslavement to our possessions, the joy of helping others, and God's approval.

11:29 One of the greatest resources God gives us is the family. Families provide acceptance, encouragement, guidance, and counsel. Bringing trouble on your family—whether through anger or through an exaggerated desire for independence—is foolish because you cut yourself off from all they provide. In your family, strive for healing, communication, and understanding.

11:30 A wise person is a model of a meaningful life. Like a tree attracts people to its shade, his or her sense of purpose attracts others who want to know how they too can find meaning. Gaining wisdom yourself, then, can be the first step in leading people to God. Leading people to God is important because it keeps us in touch with God while offering others eternal life.

11:31 Contrary to popular opinion, no one sins and gets away with it. The faithful are rewarded for their faith. The wicked are punished for their sins. Don't think for a moment that "it won't matter" or "nobody will know" or "we won't get caught" (see also 1 Peter 4:18).

12:1 If you don't want to learn, years of schooling will teach you very little. But if you want to be taught, there is no end to what you can learn. This includes being willing to accept discipline and correction and to learn from the wisdom of others. A person who refuses constructive criticism has a problem with pride. Such a person is unlikely to learn very much.

[3]A man cannot be established through wickedness,
but the righteous cannot be uprooted.

[4]A wife of noble character is her husband's crown,
but a disgraceful wife is like decay in his bones.

[5]The plans of the righteous are just,
but the advice of the wicked is deceitful.

[6]The words of the wicked lie in wait for blood,
but the speech of the upright rescues them.

[7]Wicked men are overthrown and are no more,
but the house of the righteous stands firm.

[8]A man is praised according to his wisdom,
but men with warped minds are despised.

[9]Better to be a nobody and yet have a servant
than pretend to be somebody and have no food.

[10]A righteous man cares for the needs of his animal,
but the kindest acts of the wicked are cruel.

[11]He who works his land will have abundant food,
but he who chases fantasies lacks judgment.

[12]The wicked desire the plunder of evil men,
but the root of the righteous flourishes.

[13]An evil man is trapped by his sinful talk,
but a righteous man escapes trouble.

[14]From the fruit of his lips a man is filled with good things
as surely as the work of his hands rewards him.

[15]The way of a fool seems right to him,
but a wise man listens to advice.

[16]A fool shows his annoyance at once,
but a prudent man overlooks an insult.

[17]A truthful witness gives honest testimony,
but a false witness tells lies.

[18]Reckless words pierce like a sword,
but the tongue of the wise brings healing.

[19]Truthful lips endure forever,
but a lying tongue lasts only a moment.

12:3 Ps 15:1-5
12:4 Prov 14:1; 19:13; 21:9; 27:15; 31:10; 1 Cor 11:7
12:5 Prov 16:23; Mt 12:34; 15:18
12:6 Ps 12:5; 35:11; Prov 14:3; 31:8
12:7 Isa 3:10,11; Mt 7:24-27
12:9 Lk 14:11
12:11 Prov 9:6; 14:24
12:12 Prov 1:18,19; 11:24,25; 21:10
12:13 Prov 25:18
12:14 Isa 3:10
12:15 Prov 14:12; 16:2; 21:2
12:16 Prov 19:11; 29:11
12:18 Prov 8:6,7; 15:4
12:19 Job 20:5; Prov 19:9

12:3 To be established means to be successful. Real success comes only to those who do what is right. Their efforts stand the test of time. Then, what kind of success does wickedness bring? We all know people who cheated to pass the course or to get a larger tax refund—is this not success? And what about the person who ignores his family commitments and mistreats his workers but gets ahead in business? These apparent successes are only temporary. They are bought at the expense of character. Cheaters grow more and more dishonest, and those who hurt others become callous and cruel. In the long run, evil behavior does not lead to success; it leads only to more evil. Real success maintains personal integrity. If you are not a success by God's standards, you have not achieved true success. (See the chart in chapter 19.)

12:13 Sinful talk is twisting the facts to support your claims. Those who do this are likely to be trapped by their own lies. But for someone who always tells the truth, the facts—plain and unvarnished—give an unshakable defense. If you find you always have to defend yourself to others, maybe your honesty is less than it should be. (See the chart in chapter 20.)

12:16 When someone annoys or insults you, it is natural to retaliate. But this solves nothing and only encourages trouble. Instead, answer slowly and quietly. Your positive response will achieve positive results. Proverbs 15:1 says, "A gentle answer turns away wrath."

12:19 Truth is always timely; it applies today and in the future. Because it is connected with God's changeless character, it is also changeless. Think for a moment about the centuries that have passed since these proverbs were written. Consider the countless hours that have been spent carefully studying every sentence of Scripture. The Bible has withstood the test of time. Because God is truth, you can trust his Word to guide you.

12:20
Prov 2:10
26:24-26

20There is deceit in the hearts of those who plot evil,
but joy for those who promote peace.

21No harm befalls the righteous,
but the wicked have their fill of trouble.

22The LORD detests lying lips,
but he delights in men who are truthful.

23A prudent man keeps his knowledge to himself,
but the heart of fools blurts out folly.

24Diligent hands will rule,
but laziness ends in slave labor.

12:25
Prov 15:13
17:22

25An anxious heart weighs a man down,
but a kind word cheers him up.

26A righteous man is cautious in friendship,[a]
but the way of the wicked leads them astray.

27The lazy man does not roast[b] his game,
but the diligent man prizes his possessions.

28In the way of righteousness there is life;
along that path is immortality.

13

A wise son heeds his father's instruction,
but a mocker does not listen to rebuke.

2From the fruit of his lips a man enjoys good things,
but the unfaithful have a craving for violence.

13:3
Prov 18:7,21
20:19; 21:23
Jas 3:2

3He who guards his lips guards his life,
but he who speaks rashly will come to ruin.

13:4
Prov 12:11,24
14:11; 22:29

4The sluggard craves and gets nothing,
but the desires of the diligent are fully satisfied.

13:5
Prov 3:35

5The righteous hate what is false,
but the wicked bring shame and disgrace.

13:6
Ps 15:3

6Righteousness guards the man of integrity,
but wickedness overthrows the sinner.

[a] *26* Or *man is a guide to his neighbor* [b] *27* The meaning of the Hebrew for this word is uncertain.

12:21 This is another general, but not universal, truth. Although harm does befall the righteous, they are able to see opportunities in their problems and move ahead. The wicked, without God's wisdom, are ill-equipped to handle their problems. (See the notes on 3:16, 17; 10:3; 11:8 for more about general truths that are not intended as universal statements.)

12:23 Prudent people have a quiet confidence. Insecure or uncertain people feel the need to prove themselves, but prudent people don't have to prove anything. They know they are capable, so they can get on with their work. Beware of showing off. If you are modest, people may not notice you at first, but they will respect you later.

12:27 The diligent make wise use of their possessions and resources; the lazy waste them. Waste has become a way of life for many who live in a land of plenty. Waste is poor stewardship. Make good use of everything God has given you, and prize it.

12:28 For many, death is a darkened door at the end of life, a passageway to an unknown and feared destiny. But for God's people, death is a bright pathway to a new and better life. So why do we fear death? Is it because of the pain we expect, the separation from loved ones, its surprise? God can help us deal with those fears. He has shown us that death is not final, but is just another step in the eternal life we received when we followed him.

13:3 You have not mastered self-control if you do not control what you say. Words can cut and destroy. James recognized this truth when he stated, "The tongue is a small part of the body, but it makes great boasts" (James 3:5). If you want to be self-controlled, begin with your tongue. Stop and think before you react or speak. If you can control this small but powerful member, you can control the rest of your body. (See the chart in chapter 27.)

• **13:6** Living right is like posting a guard for your life. Every choice for good sets into motion other opportunities for good. Evil choices follow the same pattern, but in the opposite direction. Each decision you make to obey God's Word will bring a greater sense of order to your life, while each decision to disobey brings confusion and destruction. The right choices you make reflect your integrity. Obedience brings the greatest safety and security.

[7]One man pretends to be rich, yet has nothing;
another pretends to be poor, yet has great wealth.

[8]A man's riches may ransom his life,
but a poor man hears no threat.

[9]The light of the righteous shines brightly,
but the lamp of the wicked is snuffed out.

[10]Pride only breeds quarrels,
but wisdom is found in those who take advice.

[11]Dishonest money dwindles away,
but he who gathers money little by little makes it grow.

[12]Hope deferred makes the heart sick,
but a longing fulfilled is a tree of life.

[13]He who scorns instruction will pay for it,
but he who respects a command is rewarded.

[14]The teaching of the wise is a fountain of life,
turning a man from the snares of death.

[15]Good understanding wins favor,
but the way of the unfaithful is hard.[a]

[16]Every prudent man acts out of knowledge,
but a fool exposes his folly.

[17]A wicked messenger falls into trouble,
but a trustworthy envoy brings healing.

[18]He who ignores discipline comes to poverty and shame,
but whoever heeds correction is honored.

[19]A longing fulfilled is sweet to the soul,
but fools detest turning from evil.

[20]He who walks with the wise grows wise,
but a companion of fools suffers harm.

[21]Misfortune pursues the sinner,
but prosperity is the reward of the righteous.

[a] 15 Or *unfaithful does not endure*

13:7 Lk 12:20,21 Jas 2:5
13:9 Job 18:5; 29:3 Prov 4:18; 24:20
13:10 Prov 12:15 17:14; 19:20
13:13 2 Chron 36:16 Prov 1:25,30
13:14 Prov 8:8
13:15 Prov 3:4; 8:35
13:16 Prov 16:1,9 27:1
13:17 Prov 26:6
13:18 Prov 23:12
13:20 Prov 2:20
13:21 Ps 32:10 Isa 3:10; 47:11

•**13:10** "I was wrong" or "I need advice" are difficult phrases to utter because they require humility. Pride is an ingredient in every quarrel. It stirs up conflict and divides people. Humility, by contrast, heals. Guard against pride. If you find yourself constantly arguing, examine your life for pride. Be open to the advice of others, ask for help when you need it, and be willing to admit your mistakes.

13:13 God created us, knows us, and loves us. It only makes sense, then, to listen to his instructions and do what he says. The Bible is his unfailing word to us. It is like an owner's manual for a car. If you obey God's instructions, you will "run right" and find his kind of power to live. If you ignore them, you will have breakdowns, accidents, and failures.

13:17 In Solomon's day, a king had to rely on messengers for information about his country. These messengers had to be trustworthy. Inaccurate information could even lead to bloodshed. Reliable communication is still vital. If the message received is different from the message sent, marriages, businesses, and diplomatic relations can all break down. It is important to choose your words well and to avoid reacting until you clearly understand what the other person means.

•**13:19** Whether a "longing fulfilled" is good or bad depends on the nature of the desire. It is "sweet to the soul" to achieve worthwhile goals, but not all goals are worth pursuing. When you set your heart on something, you may lose your ability to assess it objectively. Your desire blinds your judgment, and you proceed with an unwise relationship, a wasteful purchase, or a poorly conceived plan. Faithfulness is a virtue, but stubbornness is not.

13:20 The old saying, "A rotten apple spoils the barrel" is often applied to friendships, and with good reason. Our friends and associates affect us, sometimes profoundly. Be careful whom you choose as your closest friends. Spend time with people you want to be like—because you and your friends will surely grow to resemble each other.

13:20 When most people need advice, they go to their friends first because friends accept them and usually agree with them. But that is why they may not be able to help them with difficult problems. Our friends are so much like us that they may not have any answers we haven't already heard. Instead, we should seek out older and wiser people to advise us. Wise people have experienced a lot of life—and succeeded. They are not afraid to tell the truth. Who are the wise, godly people who can warn you of the pitfalls ahead?

13:22
Ezra 9:12
Ps 37:25
Prov 28:8

[22]A good man leaves an inheritance for his children's children,
but a sinner's wealth is stored up for the righteous.

[23]A poor man's field may produce abundant food,
but injustice sweeps it away.

13:24
Prov 19:18
22:15; 23:13
Heb 12:6

[24]He who spares the rod hates his son,
but he who loves him is careful to discipline him.

[25]The righteous eat to their hearts' content,
but the stomach of the wicked goes hungry.

14:1
Prov 12:4; 21:9
27:15; 31:10

14

The wise woman builds her house,
but with her own hands the foolish one tears hers down.

14:2
Ps 92:15

[2]He whose walk is upright fears the LORD,
but he whose ways are devious despises him.

WISDOM AND FOOLISHNESS
The wise and the foolish are often contrasted in Proverbs. The characteristics, reputation, and results of each are worth knowing if wisdom is our goal.

	The Wise	*The Foolish*	
Characteristics	Help others with good advice	Lack of judgment	10:21
	Enjoy wisdom	Enjoy foolishness	10:23
	Cautious with reason	Gullible	14:15
		Avoid the wise	15:12
	Seek knowledge	Feed on foolishness	15:14
	Value wisdom above riches		16:16
	Receive life	Receive punishment	16:22
	Respond to correction	Respond to punishment	17:10
	Pursue wisdom	Pursue illusive dreams	17:24
		Blame failure on God	19:3
	Profit from correction	An example to others	19:25
		Are proud and arrogant	21:24
		Scorn good advice	23:9
		Make truth useless	26:7
		Repeat their folly	26:11
	Trust in wisdom	Trust in themselves	28:26
	Control their anger	Unleash their anger	29:11
Reputation	Admired as counselors	Beaten as servants	10:13
	Rewarded with knowledge	Inherit folly	14:18
		Cause strife and quarrels	22:10
		Receive no honor	26:1
	Keep peace	Stir up anger	29:8
Results	Stay on straight paths	Go the wrong way	15:21
		Lash out when discovered in folly	17:12
		Endangered by their words	18:6, 7
	Their wisdom conquers others' strength		21:22
	Avoid wicked paths	Walk a troublesome path	22:5
	Have great advice		24:5
		Will never be chosen as counselors	24:7
		Must be guided by hardship	26:3
		Persist in foolishness	27:22

13:23 The poor are often victims of an unjust society. A poor man's soil may be good, but unjust laws may rob him of the his own produce. This proverb does not take poverty lightly or wink at injustice; it simply describes what often occurs. We should do what we can to fight injustice of every sort. Our efforts may seem inadequate; but it is comforting to know that in the end God's justice will prevail.

13:24 It is not easy for a loving parent to discipline a child, but it is necessary. The greatest responsibility God gives parents is the nurture and guidance of their children. Lack of discipline puts parents' love in question because it shows a lack of concern for the character development of their children. Disciplining children averts long-range disaster. Without correction, children grow up with no clear understanding of right and wrong and with little direction to their lives. Don't be afraid to discipline your children. It is an act of love. Remember, however, that your efforts cannot make your children wise; they can only encourage your children to seek God's wisdom above all else!

[3]A fool's talk brings a rod to his back,
but the lips of the wise protect them.

[4]Where there are no oxen, the manger is empty,
but from the strength of an ox comes an abundant harvest.

[5]A truthful witness does not deceive,
but a false witness pours out lies.

[6]The mocker seeks wisdom and finds none,
but knowledge comes easily to the discerning.

[7]Stay away from a foolish man,
for you will not find knowledge on his lips.

[8]The wisdom of the prudent is to give thought to their ways,
but the folly of fools is deception.

[9]Fools mock at making amends for sin,
but goodwill is found among the upright.

[10]Each heart knows its own bitterness,
and no one else can share its joy.

[11]The house of the wicked will be destroyed,
but the tent of the upright will flourish.

[12]There is a way that seems right to a man,
but in the end it leads to death.

[13]Even in laughter the heart may ache,
and joy may end in grief.

[14]The faithless will be fully repaid for their ways,
and the good man rewarded for his.

[15]A simple man believes anything,
but a prudent man gives thought to his steps.

[16]A wise man fears the LORD and shuns evil,
but a fool is hotheaded and reckless.

[17]A quick-tempered man does foolish things,
and a crafty man is hated.

[18]The simple inherit folly,
but the prudent are crowned with knowledge.

[19]Evil men will bow down in the presence of the good,
and the wicked at the gates of the righteous.

14:3 Prov 24:7,9 26:9

14:5 Prov 14:25; 19:9

14:6 Prov 9:7,8 15:12,14

14:7 Prov 23:9

14:8 Prov 1:22; 10:8 12:15; 18:2 28:26

14:11 Prov 12:7,11 13:11; 22:29

14:12 Prov 16:25 Rom 6:21

14:13 Eccles 2:1

14:14 Prov 1:31 12:14,21

14:16 Prov 22:3; 27:12

14:17 Prov 12:16 14:29; 19:19 22:24,25

14:18 Prov 3:35 14:24; 16:22

14:4 When a farmer has no oxen for plowing, his food trough for the animals will be empty. It is good to be neat, but it is better to be useful. The only way to have a perfect stable is to keep all the animals out. The only way to keep your life free of people problems is to keep it free of other people. But if your life is empty of people, it is useless; and if you live only for yourself, your life loses its meaning. Instead of avoiding people, we should serve others, share the faith, and work for justice. Is your life clean, but empty? Or does it give evidence of your serving God wholeheartedly?

14:6 We all know mockers, people who scoff at every word of instruction or advice. They never find wisdom because they don't seek it seriously. Wisdom comes easily only to those who pay attention to experienced people and to God. If the wisdom you need does not come easily to you, perhaps your attitude is the barrier.

14:9 How rarely we find goodwill around us today. Angry drivers scowl at each other in the streets. People fight to be first in line. Disgruntled employers and employees both demand their rights. But the common bond of God's people should be goodwill. Those with goodwill think the best of others and assume that others have good motives and intend to do what is right. When someone crosses you, and you feel your blood pressure rising, ask yourself, "How can I show goodwill to this person?"

•**14:12** The "way that seems right" may offer many options and require few sacrifices. Easy choices, however, should make us take a second look at the options. Is this solution attractive because it allows me to be lazy? Because it doesn't ask me to change my lifestyle? Because it requires no moral restraints? The right choice often requires hard work and self-sacrifice. Don't be enticed by apparent shortcuts that seem right, but end in death.

14:20
Prov 19:4,7

20The poor are shunned even by their neighbors,
but the rich have many friends.

14:21
Ps 41:1
Prov 19:17; 28:8

21He who despises his neighbor sins,
but blessed is he who is kind to the needy.

22Do not those who plot evil go astray?
But those who plan what is good find[a] love and faithfulness.

14:23
Prov 20:13; 28:19

23All hard work brings a profit,
but mere talk leads only to poverty.

14:24
Prov 14:18
16:22

24The wealth of the wise is their crown,
but the folly of fools yields folly.

25A truthful witness saves lives,
but a false witness is deceitful.

14:26
Ps 34:7
Prov 3:7,8,
24-26; 18:10
19:23

26He who fears the LORD has a secure fortress,
and for his children it will be a refuge.

27The fear of the LORD is a fountain of life,
turning a man from the snares of death.

14:28
1 Kgs 4:20

28A large population is a king's glory,
but without subjects a prince is ruined.

14:29
Prov 16:32
19:11; 29:11
Jas 1:19

29A patient man has great understanding,
but a quick-tempered man displays folly.

30A heart at peace gives life to the body,
but envy rots the bones.

14:31
Ps 12:5
Prov 14:21
17:5; 22:2,16
Eccles 5:8

31He who oppresses the poor shows contempt for their Maker,
but whoever is kind to the needy honors God.

32When calamity comes, the wicked are brought down,
but even in death the righteous have a refuge.

14:33
Prov 1:20; 8:4

33Wisdom reposes in the heart of the discerning
and even among fools she lets herself be known.[b]

14:34
Deut 4:6
28:1,15

34Righteousness exalts a nation,
but sin is a disgrace to any people.

35A king delights in a wise servant,
but a shameful servant incurs his wrath.

15:1
Judg 8:1-3
1 Sam 25:10-13
Prov 25:10,15

15

A gentle answer turns away wrath,
but a harsh word stirs up anger.

2The tongue of the wise commends knowledge,
but the mouth of the fool gushes folly.

[a] *22* Or *show* [b] *33* Hebrew; Septuagint and Syriac / *but in the heart of fools she is not known*

14:29 A quick temper can be like a fire out of control. It can burn us and everything in its path. Anger divides people. It pushes us into hasty decisions that only cause bitterness and guilt. Yet anger, in itself, is not wrong. Anger can be a legitimate reaction to injustice and sin. When you feel yourself getting angry, look for the cause. Are you reacting to an evil situation that you are going to set right? Or are you responding selfishly to a personal insult? Pray that God will help you control your quick temper, channeling your feelings into effective action and conquering selfish anger through humility and repentance.

14:31 God has a special concern for the poor. He insists that people who have material goods should be generous with those who are needy. Providing for the poor is not just a suggestion in the Bible; it is a command that may require a change of attitude (see Leviticus 23:22; Deuteronomy 15:7, 8; Psalms 113:5–9; 146:5–9; Isaiah 58:7; 2 Corinthians 9:9; James 2:1–9).

15:1 Have you ever tried to argue in a whisper? It is equally hard to argue with someone who insists on answering gently. On the other hand, a rising voice and harsh words almost always trigger an angry response. To turn away wrath and seek peace, gentle words are your best choice.

[3]The eyes of the LORD are everywhere,
keeping watch on the wicked and the good.

[4]The tongue that brings healing is a tree of life,
but a deceitful tongue crushes the spirit.

[5]A fool spurns his father's discipline,
but whoever heeds correction shows prudence.

[6]The house of the righteous contains great treasure,
but the income of the wicked brings them trouble.

[7]The lips of the wise spread knowledge;
not so the hearts of fools.

[8]The LORD detests the sacrifice of the wicked,
but the prayer of the upright pleases him.

[9]The LORD detests the way of the wicked
but he loves those who pursue righteousness.

[10]Stern discipline awaits him who leaves the path;
he who hates correction will die.

[11]Death and Destruction[a] lie open before the LORD—
how much more the hearts of men!

[12]A mocker resents correction;
he will not consult the wise.

[13]A happy heart makes the face cheerful,
but heartache crushes the spirit.

[14]The discerning heart seeks knowledge,
but the mouth of a fool feeds on folly.

[15]All the days of the oppressed are wretched,
but the cheerful heart has a continual feast.

[16]Better a little with the fear of the LORD
than great wealth with turmoil.

[17]Better a meal of vegetables where there is love
than a fattened calf with hatred.

[18]A hot-tempered man stirs up dissension,
but a patient man calms a quarrel.

[19]The way of the sluggard is blocked with thorns,
but the path of the upright is a highway.

15:3 1 Chron 29:17 Heb 4:13
15:5 1 Sam 2:25 Prov 10:1; 13:1 23:22
15:8 Prov 15:29 21:27 Isa 1:11
15:9,10 Ps 1:6; 146:8,9 Prov 4:18
15:11 Job 26:6 Ps 139:1
15:13 Prov 17:22 Eccles 8:1
15:14 Prov 18:15
15:16 Prov 16:8; 28:6
15:17 Prov 17:1
15:18 Prov 14:29 16:28; 26:21
15:19 Prov 22:13

[a] 11 Hebrew *Sheol and Abaddon*

15:3 At times it seems that God has let evil run rampant in the world; we wonder if he even notices it. But God sees everything clearly—both the evil actions and the evil intentions lying behind them (15:11). He is not an indifferent observer. He cares and is active in our world. Right now, his work may be unseen and unfelt, but don't give up. One day he will wipe out evil and punish the evildoers, just as he will establish the good and reward those who do his will.

15:14 What we feed our minds is just as important as what we feed our bodies. The kinds of books we read, the people we talk with, the music we listen to, and the films we watch are all part of our mental diet. Be discerning because what you feed your mind influences your total health and well-being. Thus, a strong desire to discover knowledge is a mark of wisdom.

15:15 Our attitudes color our whole personality. We cannot always choose what happens to us, but we can choose our attitude toward each situation. The secret to a cheerful heart is filling our minds with thoughts that are true, pure, and lovely; thoughts that dwell on the good things in life (Philippians 4:8). This was Paul's secret as he faced imprisonment, and it can be ours as we face the struggles of daily living. Look at your attitudes and then examine what you allow to enter your mind and what you choose to dwell on. You may need to make some changes.

• **15:17–19** The "path of the upright" doesn't always seem easy (15:19), but look at the alternatives. Hatred (15:17), dissension (15:18), and laziness (15:19) cause problems that the righteous person does not have to face. By comparison, his life is a smooth, level road because it is built on a solid foundation of love for God.

15:20 Prov 10:1; 29:3 30:17

20 A wise son brings joy to his father,
but a foolish man despises his mother.

21 Folly delights a man who lacks judgment,
but a man of understanding keeps a straight course.

15:22 Prov 11:14; 24:6

22 Plans fail for lack of counsel,
but with many advisers they succeed.

15:23 Prov 12:14 24:26; 25:11

23 A man finds joy in giving an apt reply—
and how good is a timely word!

24 The path of life leads upward for the wise
to keep him from going down to the grave.[a]

15:25 Ps 68:5; 146:9 Prov 14:11

25 The LORD tears down the proud man's house
but he keeps the widow's boundaries intact.

26 The LORD detests the thoughts of the wicked,
but those of the pure are pleasing to him.

15:27 Ex 23:8 Prov 20:21 28:16

27 A greedy man brings trouble to his family,
but he who hates bribes will live.

15:28 Prov 10:19,32 13:16; 16:23

28 The heart of the righteous weighs its answers,
but the mouth of the wicked gushes evil.

29 The LORD is far from the wicked
but he hears the prayer of the righteous.

30 A cheerful look brings joy to the heart,
and good news gives health to the bones.

15:31 Prov 8:33 13:18; 15:5 23:12

31 He who listens to a life-giving rebuke
will be at home among the wise.

32 He who ignores discipline despises himself,
but whoever heeds correction gains understanding.

15:33 Prov 1:7

33 The fear of the LORD teaches a man wisdom,[b]
and humility comes before honor.

16:1 Prov 16:9 19:21; 20:24

16 To man belong the plans of the heart,
but from the LORD comes the reply of the tongue.

2 All a man's ways seem innocent to him,
but motives are weighed by the LORD.

16:3 Prov 3:6

3 Commit to the LORD whatever you do,
and your plans will succeed.

[a] 24 Hebrew *Sheol* [b] 33 Or *Wisdom teaches the fear of the LORD*

15:22 Those with tunnel vision, people who are locked into one way of thinking, are likely to miss the right road because they have closed their minds to any new options. We need the help of those who can enlarge our vision and broaden our perspective. Seek out the advice of those who know you and have a wealth of experience. Build a network of advisers. Then be open to new ideas and be willing to weigh their suggestions carefully. Your plans will be stronger and more likely to succeed.

• **15:28** The righteous weigh their answers; the wicked don't wait to speak because they don't care about the effects of their words. It is important to have something to say, but it is equally important to weigh it first. Do you carefully plan your words, or do you pour out your thoughts without concern for their impact?

• **16:1** "From the LORD comes the reply of the tongue" means that the final outcome is in God's hands. If this is so, why make plans? In doing God's will, there must be partnership between our efforts and God's control. He wants us to use our minds, to seek the advice of others, and to plan. Nevertheless, the results are up to him.

• **16:2** People can rationalize anything if they have no standards for judging right and wrong. We can always prove that we are right. Before putting any plan into action, ask yourself these three questions: (1) Is this plan in harmony with God's truth? (2) Will it work under real-life conditions? (3) Is my attitude pleasing to God?

16:3 There are different ways to fail to commit our work to the Lord. Some people commit their work only superficially. They say the project is being done for the Lord, but in reality they are doing it for themselves. Others give God temporary control of their interests, only to take control back the moment things stop going the way they expect. Still others commit their task fully to the Lord, but put forth no effort themselves, and then they wonder why they do not succeed. Think of a specific effort in which you are involved right now. Have you committed it to the Lord?

[4]The LORD works out everything for his own ends—
even the wicked for a day of disaster.

16:4 Isa 43:7; 54:16

[5]The LORD detests all the proud of heart.
Be sure of this: They will not go unpunished.

16:5 Prov 6:16,17

[6]Through love and faithfulness sin is atoned for;
through the fear of the LORD a man avoids evil.

[7]When a man's ways are pleasing to the LORD,
he makes even his enemies live at peace with him.

16:7 2 Chron 17:10 Prov 29:25

[8]Better a little with righteousness
than much gain with injustice.

16:8 Prov 15:16; 21:6 1 Tim 6:8

[9]In his heart a man plans his course,
but the LORD determines his steps.

16:9 Ps 37:23 Prov 16:1 19:21; 20:24

[10]The lips of a king speak as an oracle,
and his mouth should not betray justice.

16:10 1 Kgs 3:28

[11]Honest scales and balances are from the LORD;
all the weights in the bag are of his making.

[12]Kings detest wrongdoing,
for a throne is established through righteousness.

16:12 Prov 14:34 25:5; 29:14

[13]Kings take pleasure in honest lips;
they value a man who speaks the truth.

16:13 Prov 22:11

[14]A king's wrath is a messenger of death,
but a wise man will appease it.

16:14 Prov 19:12; 20:2 Dan 3:13

[15]When a king's face brightens, it means life;
his favor is like a rain cloud in spring.

[16]How much better to get wisdom than gold,
to choose understanding rather than silver!

16:16 Ps 119:127

[17]The highway of the upright avoids evil;
he who guards his way guards his life.

[18]Pride goes before destruction,
a haughty spirit before a fall.

16:18 Jer 49:16

16:4 This verse doesn't mean that God created some people to be wicked, but rather that God uses even the activities of wicked people to fulfill his good purposes. God is infinite and we are finite. No matter how great our intellects, we will never be able to understand him completely. But we can accept by faith that he is all-powerful, all-loving, and all-good. We can believe that he is not the cause of evil (James 1:13, 17); and we can trust that there are no loose ends in his system of judgment. Evil is a temporary condition in the universe. One day God will destroy it. In the meantime, he uses even the evil intentions of people for his good purposes (see Genesis 50:20).

16:5 Pride is the inner voice that whispers, "My way is best." It is resisting God's leadership and believing that you are able to live without his help. Whenever you find yourself wanting to do it your way and looking down on other people, you are being pulled by pride. Only when you eliminate pride can God help you become all he meant you to be. (See the chart in chapter 19.)

16:7 We want other people to like us, and sometimes we will do almost anything to win their approval. But God tells us to put our energy into pleasing him instead. Our effort to be peacemakers will usually make us more attractive to those around us, even our enemies. But even if it doesn't, we haven't lost anything. We are still pleasing God, the only one who truly matters.

16:11 Whether we buy or sell, make a product or offer a service, we know what is honest and what is dishonest. Sometimes we feel pressure to be dishonest in order to advance ourselves or gain more profit. But if we want to obey God, there is no middle ground: God demands honesty in every business transaction. No amount of rationalizing can cover for a dishonest business practice. Honesty and fairness is not always easy, but it is what God demands. Ask him for discernment and courage to be consistently honest and fair.

16:18 Proud people take little account of their weaknesses and do not anticipate stumbling blocks. They think they are above the frailties of common people. In this state of mind they are easily tripped up. Ironically, proud people seldom realize that pride is their problem, although everyone around them is well aware of it. Ask someone you trust whether self-satisfaction has blinded you to warning signs. He or she may help you avoid a fall.

[19]Better to be lowly in spirit and among the oppressed
than to share plunder with the proud.

16:20
Ps 2:12; 34:8
Jer 17:7

[20]Whoever gives heed to instruction prospers,
and blessed is he who trusts in the LORD.

[21]The wise in heart are called discerning,
and pleasant words promote instruction.[a]

16:22
Prov 3:22
14:18,24,27

[22]Understanding is a fountain of life to those who have it,
but folly brings punishment to fools.

16:23
Ps 37:30
Prov 15:18,28

[23]A wise man's heart guides his mouth,
and his lips promote instruction.[b]

16:24
Prov 4:22
17:22; 24:13

[24]Pleasant words are a honeycomb,
sweet to the soul and healing to the bones.

[25]There is a way that seems right to a man,
but in the end it leads to death.

[26]The laborer's appetite works for him;
his hunger drives him on.

16:27
Jas 3:6

[27]A scoundrel plots evil,
and his speech is like a scorching fire.

16:28
Prov 6:14,19
18:8; 26:20

[28]A perverse man stirs up dissension,
and a gossip separates close friends.

[29]A violent man entices his neighbor
and leads him down a path that is not good.

[a]21 Or *words make a man persuasive* [b]23 Or *mouth / and makes his lips persuasive*

HOW GOD IS DESCRIBED IN PROVERBS
Proverbs is a book about wise living. It often focuses on a person's response and attitude toward God, who is the source of wisdom. And a number of proverbs point out aspects of God's character. Knowing God helps us on the way to wisdom.

God . . .	is aware of all that happens	15:3
	knows the heart of all people	15:11; 16:2; 21:2
	controls all things	16:33; 21:30
	is a place of safety	18:10
	rescues good people from danger	11:8, 21
	condemns the wicked	11:31
	delights in our prayers	15:8, 29
	loves those who obey him	15:9; 22:12
	cares for poor and needy	15:25; 22:22, 23
	purifies hearts	17:3
	hates those who do evil	17:5; 21:27; 28:9
Our Response should be . . .	to fear and reverence God	10:27; 14:26, 27; 15:16; 16:6; 19:23; 28:14
	to obey God's Word	13:13; 19:16
	to please God	21:3
	to trust God	22:17–19; 29:25

16:22 For centuries people sought a fountain of youth, a spring that promised to give eternal life and vitality. It was never found. But God's wisdom is a fountain of life that can make a person happy, healthy, and alive forever. How? When we live by God's Word, he washes away the deadly effects of sin (see Titus 3:4–8), and the hope of eternal life with him gives us a joyful perspective on our present life. The fountain of youth was only a dream, but the fountain of life is reality. The choice is yours. You can be enlightened by God's wisdom, or you can be dragged down by the weight of your own foolishness.

16:26 "The laborer's appetite works for him" means that no matter how much difficulty or drudgery we may find in our work, our appetite is an incentive to keep going. Hunger makes us work to satisfy it.

[30]He who winks with his eye is plotting perversity;
he who purses his lips is bent on evil.

[31]Gray hair is a crown of splendor;
it is attained by a righteous life.

16:31 Mt 5:36

[32]Better a patient man than a warrior,
a man who controls his temper than one who takes a city.

16:32 Prov 14:29 15:18; 19:11

[33]The lot is cast into the lap,
but its every decision is from the LORD.

17

Better a dry crust with peace and quiet
than a house full of feasting,[a] with strife.

17:1 Prov 15:17; 21:9

[2]A wise servant will rule over a disgraceful son,
and will share the inheritance as one of the brothers.

[3]The crucible for silver and the furnace for gold,
but the LORD tests the heart.

17:3 1 Chron 29:17

[4]A wicked man listens to evil lips;
a liar pays attention to a malicious tongue.

17:4 Prov 1:10; 16:29

[5]He who mocks the poor shows contempt for their Maker;
whoever gloats over disaster will not go unpunished.

17:5 Job 31:29 Prov 24:17

[6]Children's children are a crown to the aged,
and parents are the pride of their children.

17:6 Gen 48:11 Ps 127:3-5 Prov 13:22

[7]Arrogant[b] lips are unsuited to a fool—
how much worse lying lips to a ruler!

17:7 Prov 12:22

[8]A bribe is a charm to the one who gives it;
wherever he turns, he succeeds.

[9]He who covers over an offense promotes love,
but whoever repeats the matter separates close friends.

17:9 Prov 10:12

[10]A rebuke impresses a man of discernment
more than a hundred lashes a fool.

17:10 Prov 9:8; 13:1

[a] 1 Hebrew *sacrifices* [b] 7 Or *Eloquent*

16:31 The Hebrews believed that a long life was a sign of God's blessing; therefore, gray hair and old age were good. While young people glory in their strength, old people can rejoice in their years of experience and practical wisdom. Gray hair is not a sign of disgrace to be covered over; it is a crown of splendor.

16:32 Self-control is superior to conquest. Success in business, school, or home life can be ruined by one who has lost control of his or her temper. So it is a great personal victory to control your temper. When you feel yourself ready to explode, remember losing control may cause you to forfeit what you want the most.

16:33 The lot was almost always used in ceremonial settings and was the common method for determining God's will. Several important events occurred by lot, including the identification of Achan as the man who had sinned (Joshua 7:14), the division of the promised land among the tribes (Joshua 14:2), and the selection of the first king for the nation (1 Samuel 10:16–26).

17:3 It takes intense heat to purify gold and silver. Similarly, it often takes the heat of trials for the Christian to be purified. Through trials, God shows us what is in us and clears out anything that gets in the way of complete trust in him. Peter says, "These have come so that your faith—of greater worth than gold, which perishes even though refined by fire—may be proved genuine and may result in praise, glory and honor when Jesus Christ is revealed" (1 Peter 1:7). So when tough times come your way, realize that God wants to use them to refine your faith and purify your heart.

•**17:5** Few acts are as cruel as making fun of the less fortunate, but many people do this because it makes them feel good to be better off or more successful than someone else. Mocking the poor is mocking the God who made them. We also ridicule God when we mock the weak, or those who are different, or anyone else. When you catch yourself putting down others just for fun, stop and think about who created them.

17:8 Solomon is not condoning bribery (see 17:15, 23), but he is making an observation about the way the world operates. Bribes may get people what they want, but the Bible clearly condemns using them (Exodus 23:8; Proverbs 17:23; Matthew 28:11–15).

17:9 This proverb is saying that we should be willing to forgive others' sins against us. "Covering over offenses" is necessary to any relationship. It is tempting, especially in an argument, to bring up all the mistakes the other person has ever made. Love, however, keeps its mouth shut—difficult though that may be. Try never to bring anything into an argument that is unrelated to the topic being discussed. As we grow to be like Christ, we will acquire God's ability to forget the confessed sins of the past.

[11]An evil man is bent only on rebellion;
a merciless official will be sent against him.

[12]Better to meet a bear robbed of her cubs
than a fool in his folly.

17:13
Prov 13:21

[13]If a man pays back evil for good,
evil will never leave his house.

17:14
Prov 20:3; 25:8

[14]Starting a quarrel is like breaching a dam;
so drop the matter before a dispute breaks out.

17:15
Prov 24:24

[15]Acquitting the guilty and condemning the innocent—
the LORD detests them both.

[16]Of what use is money in the hand of a fool,
since he has no desire to get wisdom?

17:17
Prov 18:24

[17]A friend loves at all times,
and a brother is born for adversity.

17:18
Prov 6:1; 11:15

[18]A man lacking in judgment strikes hands in pledge
and puts up security for his neighbor.

17:19
Prov 29:22,23

[19]He who loves a quarrel loves sin;
he who builds a high gate invites destruction.

[20]A man of perverse heart does not prosper;
he whose tongue is deceitful falls into trouble.

17:21
Prov 10:1
17:25; 19:13

[21]To have a fool for a son brings grief;
there is no joy for the father of a fool.

17:22
Prov 15:13

[22]A cheerful heart is good medicine,
but a crushed spirit dries up the bones.

17:23
Ex 23:8

[23]A wicked man accepts a bribe in secret
to pervert the course of justice.

[24]A discerning man keeps wisdom in view,
but a fool's eyes wander to the ends of the earth.

17:25
Prov 10:1

[25]A foolish son brings grief to his father
and bitterness to the one who bore him.

[26]It is not good to punish an innocent man,
or to flog officials for their integrity.

17:27
Prov 10:19
Jas 1:19

[27]A man of knowledge uses words with restraint,
and a man of understanding is even-tempered.

[28]Even a fool is thought wise if he keeps silent,
and discerning if he holds his tongue.

17:17 What kind of friend are you? There is a vast difference between knowing someone well and being a true friend. The greatest evidence of genuine friendship is loyalty (loving "at all times") —being available to help in times of distress or personal struggles. Too many people are fair-weather friends. They stick around when the friendship helps them and leave when they're not getting anything out of the relationship. Think of your friends and assess your loyalty to them. Be the kind of true friend the Bible encourages.

• **17:22** To be cheerful is to be ready to greet others with a welcome, a word of encouragement, an enthusiasm for the task at hand, and a positive outlook on the future. Such people are as welcome as pain-relieving medicine.

17:24 While there is something to be said for having big dreams, this proverb points out the folly of chasing fantasies (having eyes that wander "to the ends of the earth," see 12:11). How much better to align your goals with God's, being the kind of person he wants you to be! Such goals (wisdom, honesty, patience, love) may not seem exciting, but they will determine your eternal future. Take time to think about your dreams and goals, and make sure they cover the really important areas of life.

• **17:27, 28** This proverb highlights several benefits of keeping quiet: (1) it is the best policy if you have nothing worthwhile to say; (2) it allows you the opportunity to listen and learn; and (3) it gives you something in common with those who are wiser. Make sure to pause to think and to listen so that when you do speak, you will have something important to say.

18 An unfriendly man pursues selfish ends;
he defies all sound judgment.

[2]A fool finds no pleasure in understanding
but delights in airing his own opinions.

[3]When wickedness comes, so does contempt,
and with shame comes disgrace.

[4]The words of a man's mouth are deep waters,
but the fountain of wisdom is a bubbling brook.

[5]It is not good to be partial to the wicked
or to deprive the innocent of justice.

18:5
Prov 17:15
24:23

[6]A fool's lips bring him strife,
and his mouth invites a beating.

18:6
Prov 10:14; 13:3

[7]A fool's mouth is his undoing,
and his lips are a snare to his soul.

[8]The words of a gossip are like choice morsels;
they go down to a man's inmost parts.

18:8
Lev 19:16
Prov 11:13

[9]One who is slack in his work
is brother to one who destroys.

[10]The name of the LORD is a strong tower;
the righteous run to it and are safe.

18:10
2 Sam 22:2
Ps 61:3; 91:2
Prov 29:25

[11]The wealth of the rich is their fortified city;
they imagine it an unscalable wall.

18:11
Prov 10:15

[12]Before his downfall a man's heart is proud,
but humility comes before honor.

18:12
Prov 11:2
16:18; 29:23

[13]He who answers before listening—
that is his folly and his shame.

18:13
Prov 20:25
Jn 7:51

[14]A man's spirit sustains him in sickness,
but a crushed spirit who can bear?

[15]The heart of the discerning acquires knowledge;
the ears of the wise seek it out.

18:15
Prov 15:14; 23:23

[16]A gift opens the way for the giver
and ushers him into the presence of the great.

18:16
Gen 32:20
1 Sam 25:27
Prov 17:8

[17]The first to present his case seems right,
till another comes forward and questions him.

[18]Casting the lot settles disputes
and keeps strong opponents apart.

18:18
Prov 16:33

[19]An offended brother is more unyielding than a fortified city,
and disputes are like the barred gates of a citadel.

18:19
2 Cor 6:3

• **18:8** It is as hard to refuse to listen to gossip as it is to turn down a delicious dessert. Taking just one morsel of either one creates a taste for more. You can resist rumors the same way a determined dieter resists candy—never even open the box. If you don't nibble on the first bite of gossip, you can't take the second and the third.

18:11 In imagining that his wealth is his strongest defense, the rich person is sadly mistaken. Money cannot provide safety—there are too many ways for it to lose its power. The government may cease to back it; thieves may steal it; inflation may rob it of all value. But God never loses his power. He is always dependable. What do you look to for security and safety—uncertain wealth or God who is always faithful?

18:13, 15, 17 In these concise statements, the writer gives three basic principles for making sound decisions: (1) get the facts before answering; (2) be open to new ideas; (3) make sure you hear both sides of the story before judging. All three principles center around seeking additional information. This is difficult work, but the only alternative is prejudice—judging before getting the facts.

[20]From the fruit of his mouth a man's stomach is filled;
with the harvest from his lips he is satisfied.

18:21 Prov 13:3 Mt 12:37

[21]The tongue has the power of life and death,
and those who love it will eat its fruit.

18:22 Prov 12:4 19:14; 31:10-31

[22]He who finds a wife finds what is good
and receives favor from the LORD.

18:23 2 Chron 10:13 Prov 19:7 Jas 2:3

[23]A poor man pleads for mercy,
but a rich man answers harshly.

18:24 Prov 14:20 19:4,6

[24]A man of many companions may come to ruin,
but there is a friend who sticks closer than a brother.

19 Better a poor man whose walk is blameless
than a fool whose lips are perverse.

[2]It is not good to have zeal without knowledge,
nor to be hasty and miss the way.

19:3 Isa 8:21

[3]A man's own folly ruins his life,
yet his heart rages against the LORD.

[4]Wealth brings many friends,
but a poor man's friend deserts him.

19:5 Ex 23:1

[5]A false witness will not go unpunished,
and he who pours out lies will not go free.

HUMILITY AND PRIDE
Proverbs is direct and forceful in rejecting pride. The proud attitude heads the list of seven things God hates (6:16–17). The harmful results of pride are constantly contrasted with humility and its benefits.

Results of . . .	*Humility*	*Pride*	
	Leads to wisdom	Leads to disgrace	11:2
	Takes advice	Produces quarrels	13:10
	Leads to honor		15:33
		Leads to punishment	16:5
		Leads to destruction	16:18
	Ends in honor	Ends in downfall	18:12
	Brings one to honor	Brings one low	29:23

18:22 Today's emphasis on individual freedom is misguided. Strong individuals are important, but so are strong marriages. God created marriage for our enjoyment and he pronounced it good. This is one of many passages in the Bible that show marriage as a joyful and good creation of God (Genesis 2:21–25; Proverbs 5:15–19; John 2:1–11).

18:23 This verse does not condone insulting the poor; it is simply recording an unfortunate fact of life. It is wrong for rich people to treat the less fortunate with contempt and arrogance, and God will judge such actions severely (see 14:31).

18:24 Loneliness is everywhere—many people feel cut off and alienated from others. Being in a crowd just makes people more aware of their isolation. We all need friends who will stick close, listen, care, and offer help when it is needed—in good times and bad. It is better to have one such friend than dozens of superficial acquaintances. Instead of wishing you could find a true friend, seek to become one. There are people who need your friendship. Ask God to reveal them to you, and then take on the challenge of being a true friend.

19:1 A blameless life is far more valuable than wealth, but most people don't act as if they believe this. Afraid of not getting everything they want, they will pay any price to increase their wealth—cheating on their taxes, stealing from stores or employers, withholding tithes, refusing to give. But when we know and love God, we realize that a lower standard of living—or even poverty—is a small price to pay for personal integrity. Do your actions show that you sacrifice your integrity to increase your wealth? What changes do you need to make in order to get your priorities straight?

19:2 We often move hastily through life, rushing headlong into the unknown. Many people marry without knowing what to expect of their partner or of married life. Others try illicit sex or drugs without considering the consequences. Some plunge into jobs without evaluating whether they are suitable to that line of work. Don't rush into the unknown. Be sure you understand what you're getting into and where you want to go before you take the first step. And if it still seems unknown, be sure you're following God.

[6]Many curry favor with a ruler,
and everyone is the friend of a man who gives gifts.

[7]A poor man is shunned by all his relatives—
how much more do his friends avoid him!
Though he pursues them with pleading,
they are nowhere to be found.[a]

19:7
Prov 18:23

[8]He who gets wisdom loves his own soul;
he who cherishes understanding prospers.

19:8
Prov 16:20
8:35,36

[9]A false witness will not go unpunished,
and he who pours out lies will perish.

[10]It is not fitting for a fool to live in luxury—
how much worse for a slave to rule over princes!

19:10
Prov 26:1

[11]A man's wisdom gives him patience;
it is to his glory to overlook an offense.

19:11
Prov 14:29
Col 4:6

[12]A king's rage is like the roar of a lion,
but his favor is like dew on the grass.

19:12
Prov 16:14,15

[13]A foolish son is his father's ruin,
and a quarrelsome wife is like a constant dripping.

19:13
Prov 12:4
15:20; 17:25
21:9,19

[14]Houses and wealth are inherited from parents,
but a prudent wife is from the LORD.

[15]Laziness brings on deep sleep,
and the shiftless man goes hungry.

19:15
Prov 6:9; 16:26
24:33

[16]He who obeys instructions guards his life,
but he who is contemptuous of his ways will die.

19:16
Prov 16:17

[17]He who is kind to the poor lends to the LORD,
and he will reward him for what he has done.

19:17
Deut 15:7
Prov 14:31
28:27

[18]Discipline your son, for in that there is hope;
do not be a willing party to his death.

19:18
Prov 13:24
Heb 12:6

[19]A hot-tempered man must pay the penalty;
if you rescue him, you will have to do it again.

19:19
Prov 12:16
14:17; 15:18

[20]Listen to advice and accept instruction,
and in the end you will be wise.

[21]Many are the plans in a man's heart,
but it is the LORD's purpose that prevails.

[22]What a man desires is unfailing love[b];
better to be poor than a liar.

[23]The fear of the LORD leads to life:
Then one rests content, untouched by trouble.

19:23
Ps 25:13
Prov 14:27; 22:3
1 Tim 4:8

[a] *7* The meaning of the Hebrew for this sentence is uncertain. [b] *22* Or *A man's greed is his shame*

19:8 Is it good to love yourself? Yes, when your soul is at stake! This proverb does not condone the self-centered person who loves and protects his or her selfish interests and will do anything to serve them. Instead it encourages those who really care about themselves enough to seek wisdom.

•**19:16** The instructions we are told to obey are those found in God's Word—both the Ten Commandments (Exodus 20) and other passages of instruction. To obey what God teaches in the Bible is self-preserving. To disobey is self-destructive.

19:17 Here God identifies with the poor as Jesus does in Matthew 25:31–46. As our Creator, God values all of us, whether we are poor or rich. When we help the poor, we show honor both to the Creator and to his creation. God accepts our help as if we had offered it directly to him.

19:23 Those who fear the Lord are "untouched by trouble" because of their healthy habits, their beneficial life-style, and sometimes through God's direct intervention. Nevertheless, the fear of the Lord does not always protect us from trouble in this life: evil things still happen to people who love God. This verse is not a universal promise, but a general guideline. It describes what would happen if this world were sinless, and what will happen in the new earth, when faithful believers will be under God's protection forever. (See the note on 3:16, 17 for more about this concept.)

19:25 Prov 9:7,8 19:29; 21:11

19:26 Prov 20:20

19:29 Prov 9:12 19:9,25; 26:3

20:1 Prov 31:4

20:2 Prov 16:14

20:3 Prov 14:29 16:32; 19:11

24The sluggard buries his hand in the dish;
he will not even bring it back to his mouth!

25Flog a mocker, and the simple will learn prudence;
rebuke a discerning man, and he will gain knowledge.

26He who robs his father and drives out his mother
is a son who brings shame and disgrace.

27Stop listening to instruction, my son,
and you will stray from the words of knowledge.

28A corrupt witness mocks at justice,
and the mouth of the wicked gulps down evil.

29Penalties are prepared for mockers,
and beatings for the backs of fools.

20

Wine is a mocker and beer a brawler;
whoever is led astray by them is not wise.

2A king's wrath is like the roar of a lion;
he who angers him forfeits his life.

3It is to a man's honor to avoid strife,
but every fool is quick to quarrel.

4A sluggard does not plow in season;
so at harvest time he looks but finds nothing.

5The purposes of a man's heart are deep waters,
but a man of understanding draws them out.

HOW TO SUCCEED IN GOD'S EYES
Proverbs notes two significant by-products of wise living: success and good reputation. Several verses also point out what causes failure and poor reputation.

Qualities that promote success and a good reputation:	
Righteousness	10:7; 12:3; 28:12
Hating what is false	13:5
Commiting all work to the Lord	16:3
Using words with restraint; having a settled mind	17:27, 28
Loving wisdom and understanding	19:8
Humility and fear of the Lord	22:4
Willingness to confess and renounce sin	28:13
Qualities that prevent success and cause a bad reputation:	
Wickedness	10:7; 12:3; 28:12
Seeking honor	25:27
Hatred	26:24–26
Praising oneself	27:2
Concealing sin	28:13

Other verses dealing with one's reputation are: 11:10, 16; 14:3; 19:10; 22:1; 23:17, 18; 24:13–14

19:24 "Buries his hand in the dish" refers to the custom of eating where a dish would be passed and people would reach in and get food for themselves. This proverb is saying that some people are so lazy that they won't even feed themselves.

•**19:25** There is a great difference between the person who learns from criticism and the person who refuses to accept correction. How we respond to criticism determines whether or not we grow in wisdom. The next time someone criticizes you, listen carefully to all that is said. You might learn something.

20:3 A person who is truly confident of his or her strength does not need to parade it. A truly brave person does not look for chances to prove it. A resourceful woman can find a way out of a fight. A man of endurance will avoid retaliating. Foolish people find it impossible to avoid strife. Men and women of character can. What kind of person are you?

•**20:4** You've heard similar warnings: if you don't study, you'll fail the test; if you don't save, you won't have money when you need it. God wants us to anticipate future needs and prepare for them. We can't expect him to come to our rescue when we cause our own problems through lack of planning. He provides for us, but he also expects us to be responsible.

[6]Many a man claims to have unfailing love,
but a faithful man who can find?

[7]The righteous man leads a blameless life;
blessed are his children after him.

[8]When a king sits on his throne to judge,
he winnows out all evil with his eyes.

[9]Who can say, "I have kept my heart pure;
I am clean and without sin"?

[10]Differing weights and differing measures—
the LORD detests them both.

[11]Even a child is known by his actions,
by whether his conduct is pure and right.

[12]Ears that hear and eyes that see—
the LORD has made them both.

[13]Do not love sleep or you will grow poor;
stay awake and you will have food to spare.

[14]"It's no good, it's no good!" says the buyer;
then off he goes and boasts about his purchase.

[15]Gold there is, and rubies in abundance,
but lips that speak knowledge are a rare jewel.

[16]Take the garment of one who puts up security for a stranger;
hold it in pledge if he does it for a wayward woman.

[17]Food gained by fraud tastes sweet to a man,
but he ends up with a mouth full of gravel.

[18]Make plans by seeking advice;
if you wage war, obtain guidance.

[19]A gossip betrays a confidence;
so avoid a man who talks too much.

[20]If a man curses his father or mother,
his lamp will be snuffed out in pitch darkness.

[21]An inheritance quickly gained at the beginning
will not be blessed at the end.

[22]Do not say, "I'll pay you back for this wrong!"
Wait for the LORD, and he will deliver you.

[23]The LORD detests differing weights,
and dishonest scales do not please him.

20:6 Ps 12:1
20:7 Ps 37:26; 112:2
20:8 Prov 16:12
20:9 2 Chron 6:36
20:10 Prov 11:1; 20:23
20:11 Prov 21:8; Mt 7:16
20:13 Prov 6:9,10; 19:15; 24:32,33
20:16 Ex 22:26; Prov 6:1-5
20:18 Prov 11:14; Lk 14:31
20:19 Prov 11:13
20:20 Ex 21:17; Lev 20:9; Prov 19:26
20:21 Prov 28:16
20:22 Prov 24:28,29; Mt 5:39; Rom 12:17
20:23 Prov 11:1; 20:10

20:9 No one is without sin. As soon as we confess our sin and repent, sinful thoughts and actions begin to creep back into our lives. We all need ongoing cleansing, moment by moment. Thank God for providing forgiveness by his mercy when we ask for it. Make confession and repentance a regular part of your talks with God. Rely on him moment by moment for the cleansing you need.

20:23 "Differing weights" refers to the loaded scales a merchant might use in order to cheat the customers. Dishonesty is a difficult sin to avoid. It is easy to cheat if we think no one else is looking. But dishonesty affects the very core of a person. It makes him untrustworthy and untrusting. It eventually makes him unable to know himself or relate to others. Don't take dishonesty lightly. Even the smallest portion of dishonesty contains enough of the poison of deceit to kill your spiritual life. If there is any dishonesty in your life, tell God about it now.

20:24 We are often confused by the events around us. Many things we will never understand; others will fall into place in years to come as we look back and see how God was working. This proverb counsels us not to worry if we don't understand everything as it happens. Instead, we should trust that God knows what he's doing, even if his timing or design is not clear to us. See Psalm 37:23 for a reassuring promise of God's direction in your life.

20:24
Gen 50:20
1 Kgs 12:15
Ps 37:23

[24]A man's steps are directed by the LORD.
How then can anyone understand his own way?

[25]It is a trap for a man to dedicate something rashly
and only later to consider his vows.

[26]A wise king winnows out the wicked;
he drives the threshing wheel over them.

[27]The lamp of the LORD searches the spirit of a man[a];
it searches out his inmost being.

20:28
Prov 29:14

[28]Love and faithfulness keep a king safe;
through love his throne is made secure.

20:29
Prov 16:31

[29]The glory of young men is their strength,
gray hair the splendor of the old.

[30]Blows and wounds cleanse away evil,
and beatings purge the inmost being.

[a] 27 Or *The spirit of man is the LORD's lamp*

HONESTY AND DISHONESTY
Proverbs tells us plainly that God despises all forms of dishonesty. Not only does God hate dishonesty, but we are told that it works against us—others no longer trust us, and we cannot even enjoy our dishonest gains. It is wiser to be honest because "a righteous man escapes trouble" (12:13).

Others' Opinion	
Leaders value those who speak the truth.	16:13
Most people will appreciate truth in the end more than flattery.	28:23
Quality of life	
The righteous person's plans are just.	12:5
Truthful witnesses save lives.	14:25
The children of the righteous are blessed.	20:7
Short-term results	
Ill-gotten treasure is of no value.	10:2
The righteous are rescued from trouble.	11:8
The evil are trapped by sinful talk.	12:13
Fraudulent gain is sweet for awhile.	20:17
Long-term results	
The upright are guided by integrity.	11:3
Truthful lips endure.	12:19
Riches gained quickly don't last.	20:21
Riches gained dishonestly don't last.	21:6
The blameless are kept safe.	28:18
God's Opinion	
God delights in honesty.	11:1
God delights in those who are truthful.	12:22
God detests unjust measures.	20:10
God is pleased when we do what is right and just.	21:3

20:25 To dedicate something meant that you intended to give it as an offering to God. *Dedicated* means set apart for religious use. This proverb points out the evil of making a vow rashly and then reconsidering it. God takes vows seriously and requires that they be carried out (Deuteronomy 23:21–23). We often have good intentions when making a vow because we want to show God that we are determined to please him. Jesus, however, says it is better not to make promises to God because he knows how difficult they are to keep (Matthew 5:33–37). If you still feel it is important to make a vow, make sure that you weigh the consequences of breaking that vow. (In Judges 11, Jephthah made a rash promise to sacrifice the first thing he saw on his return home. As it happened, he saw his daughter first.) It is better not to make promises than to make them and then later want to change them. It is better still to count the cost beforehand and then to fulfill them. (For a list of other Bible people who made rash vows, see the chart in Judges 11.)

20:27 God has given each of us a conscience ("the spirit") to tell us right from wrong. Without it, we would be unaware of the harm caused by certain actions, and we would not know how to do good either. The spirit searches us and exposes our hidden motives. Because our consciences are not perfect, we need the additional light of God's Word (see Psalm 119:105). The best way to stay on God's path is to use both lights at once—our spirits exposing our motives and the Bible directing our steps.

21

The king's heart is in the hand of the LORD;
he directs it like a watercourse wherever he pleases.

[2]All a man's ways seem right to him,
but the LORD weighs the heart.

[3]To do what is right and just
is more acceptable to the LORD than sacrifice.

[4]Haughty eyes and a proud heart,
the lamp of the wicked, are sin!

[5]The plans of the diligent lead to profit
as surely as haste leads to poverty.

[6]A fortune made by a lying tongue
is a fleeting vapor and a deadly snare.[a]

[7]The violence of the wicked will drag them away,
for they refuse to do what is right.

21:1 Ezra 6:21,22 Prov 16:1,9

21:2 Prov 16:2 Lk 16:15

21:3 Ps 50:8,9 Prov 15:8

21:4 Prov 6:17; 30:13 Lk 11:34

[a] 6 Some Hebrew manuscripts, Septuagint and Vulgate; most Hebrew manuscripts *vapor for those who seek death*

RIGHTEOUSNESS

Proverbs often compares the life-styles of the wicked and the righteous, and makes a strong case for living by God's pattern. The advantages of righteous living and the disadvantages of wicked living are pointed out. The kind of person we decide to be will affect every area of our lives.

	Righteous	*Wicked*	*References*
Outlook on life	Hopeful	Fearful	10:24
	Concerned about the welfare of God's creation	Even their kindness is cruel	12:10
	Understand justice	Don't understand justice	28:5
Response to life	Covered with blessings	Covered with violence	10:6
		Bent on evil	16:30
	Give thought to their ways	Put up a bold front	21:29
	Persevere against evil	Brought down by calamity	24:15, 16
		Hate those with integrity	29:10
How they are seen by others	Are appreciated	Do not endure	13:15
		Lead others into sin	16:29
	Conduct is upright	Conduct is devious	21:8
	Are not to desire the company of godless people	Plot violence	24:1, 2
	Others are glad when they triumph	Others hide when they rise to power	28:12
	Care for the poor	Unconcerned about the poor	29:7
	Detest the dishonest	Detest the upright	29:27
Quality of life	Stand firm	Swept away	10:25
	Delivered by righteousness	Trapped by evil desires	11:6

21:1 In Solomon's day, kings possessed absolute authority and were often considered like gods. This proverb shows that God, not earthly rulers, has ultimate authority over world politics. Although they may not have realized it, the earth's most powerful kings have always been under God's control. (See Isaiah 10:5–8 for an example of a king who was used for God's purposes.)

21:2 People can find an excuse for doing almost anything, but God looks behind the excuse to the motives of the heart. We often have to make choices in areas where the right action is difficult to discern. We can help ourselves make such decisions by trying to identify our motives first and then asking, "Would God be pleased with my real reasons for doing this?" God is not pleased when we do good deeds only to receive something in return.

21:3 Sacrifices and offerings are not bribes to make God overlook

[8]The way of the guilty is devious,
but the conduct of the innocent is upright.

21:9 Prov 19:13 21:19

[9]Better to live on a corner of the roof
than share a house with a quarrelsome wife.

[10]The wicked man craves evil;
his neighbor gets no mercy from him.

21:11 Prov 9:9; 15:14 19:25

[11]When a mocker is punished, the simple gain wisdom;
when a wise man is instructed, he gets knowledge.

[12]The Righteous One[a] takes note of the house of the wicked
and brings the wicked to ruin.

21:13 Prov 24:11,12 Mt 18:30-34 Lk 16:19-31 1 Jn 3:17

[13]If a man shuts his ears to the cry of the poor,
he too will cry out and not be answered.

[14]A gift given in secret soothes anger,
and a bribe concealed in the cloak pacifies great wrath.

[a] *12* Or *The righteous man*

AND WICKEDNESS

	Righteous	*Wicked*	*References*
	No real harm befalls them	Constant trouble befalls them	12:21
Quality of life (cont.)	Income results in treasure	Income results in trouble	15:6
	Avoid evil		16:17
		Fall into constant trouble	17:20
	Are bold as lions	Are fearful constantly	28:1
	Will be kept safe	Will suddenly fall	28:18
Short-term results	Walk securely	Will be found out	10:9
	Rewarded with prosperity	Pursued by misfortune	13:21
Long-term results	God protects them	God destroys them	10:29
		Will be punished for rebellion	17:11
Eternal expectations	Never uprooted	Never remain	10:30
	Earn a sure reward	Earn deceptive wages	11:18
	Attain life	Go to death	11:19
	End only in good	End only in wrath	11:23
	Shall stand	Shall perish	12:7
	Have a refuge when they die	Will be brought down by calamity	14:32
God's opinion of them	Delight in the good	Detest the perverse	11:20
	Evil people shall bow to them	They shall bow to the righteous	14:19

our character faults. If our personal and business dealings are not characterized by justice, no amount of generosity when the offering plate is passed will make up for it.

21:5 Faithful completion of mundane tasks is a great accomplishment. Such work is patiently carried out according to a plan. Diligence is a result of strong character. Don't look for quick and easy answers. Be a diligent servant of God.

• **21:11, 12** It is usually better to learn from the mistakes of others than from our own. We can do this by listening to their advice. Take counsel from others instead of plunging ahead and learning the hard way.

21:13 We should work to meet the needs of the poor and protect their rights—we may be in need of such services ourselves someday.

[15]When justice is done, it brings joy to the righteous
but terror to evildoers.

[16]A man who strays from the path of understanding
comes to rest in the company of the dead.

[17]He who loves pleasure will become poor;
whoever loves wine and oil will never be rich.

[18]The wicked become a ransom for the righteous,
and the unfaithful for the upright.

[19]Better to live in a desert
than with a quarrelsome and ill-tempered wife.

[20]In the house of the wise are stores of choice food and oil,
but a foolish man devours all he has.

[21]He who pursues righteousness and love
finds life, prosperity[a] and honor.

[22]A wise man attacks the city of the mighty
and pulls down the stronghold in which they trust.

[23]He who guards his mouth and his tongue
keeps himself from calamity.

[24]The proud and arrogant man—"Mocker" is his name;
he behaves with overweening pride.

[25]The sluggard's craving will be the death of him,
because his hands refuse to work.
[26]All day long he craves for more,
but the righteous give without sparing.

[27]The sacrifice of the wicked is detestable—
how much more so when brought with evil intent!

[28]A false witness will perish,
and whoever listens to him will be destroyed forever.[b]

[29]A wicked man puts up a bold front,
but an upright man gives thought to his ways.

[30]There is no wisdom, no insight, no plan
that can succeed against the LORD.

[31]The horse is made ready for the day of battle,
but victory rests with the LORD.

[a] 21 Or *righteousness* [b] 28 Or */ but the words of an obedient man will live on*

21:17
Prov 23:19-21

21:18
Prov 11:8
Isa 43:3,4

21:19
Prov 19:13; 21:9

21:20
Prov 8:21

21:21
Prov 2:10,21
3:16; 11:19

21:22
2 Sam 5:6-9
Prov 24:5
Eccles 9:15

21:23
Prov 13:3
Jas 3:2

21:24
Ps 1:1
Prov 13:1; 14:6

21:25
Prov 10:4; 12:24

21:30
Isa 8:9; 14:27
Acts 5:38,39

21:31
Isa 31:1-3
1 Cor 15:57

21:20 This proverb is about saving for the future. Easy credit has many people living on the edge of bankruptcy. The desire to keep up and accumulate more pushes them to spend every penny they earn, and they stretch their credit to the limit. But anyone who spends all he has is spending more than he can afford. A wise man puts money aside for when he may have less. God approves of foresight and restraint. God's people need to examine their lifestyles to see whether their spending is God-pleasing or merely self-pleasing.

21:27 The kind of worship ("sacrifice") described in this proverb is no better than a bribe. How do people try to bribe God? They may go to church, tithe, or volunteer, not because of their love and devotion to God, but because they hope God will bless them in return. But God has made it very clear that he desires obedience and love more than religious ritual (see 21:3; 1 Samuel 15:22). God does not want our sacrifices of time, energy, and money alone; he wants our hearts—our complete love and devotion. We may be able to bribe people (21:14), but we cannot bribe God.

21:31 This proverb refers to preparing for battle. All our preparation for any task is useless without God. But even with God's help we still must do our part and prepare. His control of the outcome does not negate our responsibilities. God may want you to produce a great book, but you must learn to write. God may want to use you in foreign missions, but you must learn the language. God will accomplish his purposes, and he will be able to use you if you have done your part by being well prepared.

22

A good name is more desirable than great riches;
to be esteemed is better than silver or gold.

22:2 Prov 14:31 29:13

[2]Rich and poor have this in common:
The LORD is the Maker of them all.

22:3 Prov 14:15

[3]A prudent man sees danger and takes refuge,
but the simple keep going and suffer for it.

22:4 Prov 3:16; 4:4

[4]Humility and the fear of the LORD
bring wealth and honor and life.

22:5 Prov 13:9,15

[5]In the paths of the wicked lie thorns and snares,
but he who guards his soul stays far from them.

22:6 Ps 78:4 Eph 6:4

[6]Train[a] a child in the way he should go,
and when he is old he will not turn from it.

22:7 Prov 22:15

[7]The rich rule over the poor,
and the borrower is servant to the lender.

22:8 Prov 24:16

[8]He who sows wickedness reaps trouble,
and the rod of his fury will be destroyed.

22:9 2 Cor 9:6

[9]A generous man will himself be blessed,
for he shares his food with the poor.

[10]Drive out the mocker, and out goes strife;
quarrels and insults are ended.

22:11 Prov 14:35 16:15; 22:29 Mt 5:8

[11]He who loves a pure heart and whose speech is gracious
will have the king for his friend.

[12]The eyes of the LORD keep watch over knowledge,
but he frustrates the words of the unfaithful.

[13]The sluggard says, "There is a lion outside!"
or, "I will be murdered in the streets!"

22:14 Prov 5:3; 23:26

[14]The mouth of an adulteress is a deep pit;
he who is under the LORD's wrath will fall into it.

22:15 Prov 13:24

[15]Folly is bound up in the heart of a child,
but the rod of discipline will drive it far from him.

[a]6 Or *Start*

22:4 This is a general observation that would have been especially applicable to an obedient Israelite living in Solomon's God-fearing kingdom. Nevertheless, some have been martyrs at a young age, and some have given away all their wealth for the sake of God's kingdom. The book of Proverbs describes life the way it should be. It does not dwell on the exceptions. (For more on this concept, see the note on 3:16, 17.)

22:6 "In the way he should go" is literally, "according to his [the child's] way." It is natural to want to bring up all our children alike or train them the same way. This verse implies that parents should discern the individuality and special strengths that God has given each one. While we should not condone or excuse self-will, each child has natural inclinations that parents can develop. By talking to teachers, other parents, and grandparents, we can better discern and develop the individual capabilities of each child.

• **22:6** Many parents want to make all the choices for their child, but this hurts him in the long run. When parents teach a child how to make decisions, they don't have to watch every step he takes. They know he will remain on the right path because he has made the choice himself. Train your children to choose the right way.

22:7 Does this mean we should never borrow? No, but it warns us never to take on a loan without carefully examining our ability to repay it. A loan we can handle is enabling; a loan we can't handle is enslaving. The borrower must realize that until the loan is repaid, he is a servant to the individual or institution that made it.

22:12 "Knowledge" also refers to those who live right and speak the truth. The unfaithful may seem to have an easier time of it, but in the long run their plans fail and their lives amount to nothing.

22:13 This proverb refers to an excuse a lazy person might use to avoid going to work. The excuse sounds silly to us, but that's often how our excuses sound to others. Don't rationalize laziness. Take your responsibilities seriously and get to work.

• **22:15** Young children often do foolish and dangerous things simply because they don't understand the consequences. Wisdom and common sense are not transferred by just being a good example. The wisdom a child learns must be taught consciously. "The rod of discipline" stands for all forms of discipline or training. Just as God trains and corrects us to make us better, so parents must discipline their children to make them learn the difference between right and wrong. To see how God corrects us, read 3:11, 12.

16He who oppresses the poor to increase his wealth
and he who gives gifts to the rich—both come to poverty.

22:16 Job 20:19 Prov 14:31; 28:3

Sayings of the Wise

17Pay attention and listen to the sayings of the wise;
apply your heart to what I teach,
18for it is pleasing when you keep them in your heart
and have all of them ready on your lips.
19So that your trust may be in the LORD,
I teach you today, even you.
20Have I not written thirty[a] sayings for you,
sayings of counsel and knowledge,
21teaching you true and reliable words,
so that you can give sound answers
to him who sent you?

22:17 Prov 1:7; 2:1,2

22Do not exploit the poor because they are poor
and do not crush the needy in court,
23for the LORD will take up their case
and will plunder those who plunder them.

24Do not make friends with a hot-tempered man,
do not associate with one easily angered,
25or you may learn his ways
and get yourself ensnared.

22:24 Prov 1:15; 14:7 29:22

26Do not be a man who strikes hands in pledge
or puts up security for debts;
27if you lack the means to pay,
your very bed will be snatched from under you.

22:26 Ex 22:26 Prov 6:1-5 20:16

28Do not move an ancient boundary stone
set up by your forefathers.

22:28 Deut 19:14 27:17 Prov 23:10,11

29Do you see a man skilled in his work?
He will serve before kings;
he will not serve before obscure men.

22:29 Prov 27:18

23 When you sit to dine with a ruler,
note well what[b] is before you,
2and put a knife to your throat
if you are given to gluttony.
3Do not crave his delicacies,
for that food is deceptive.

23:3 Ps 141:4 Prov 23:6

[a] 20 Or *not formerly written;* or *not written excellent* [b] 1 Or *who*

22:22, 23 This proverb is a message of hope to people who must live and work under unjust authoritarian leaders. It is also a warning to those who enjoy ruling with an iron hand. Sometimes God intervenes and directly destroys tyrants. More often, he uses other rulers to overthrow them or their own oppressed people to rebel against them. If you are in a position of authority at church, work, or home, remember what happens to tyrants. Leadership through kindness is more effective and longer lasting than leadership by force.

22:24, 25 People tend to become like those with whom they spend a lot of time. Even the negative characteristics sometimes rub off. The Bible exhorts us to be cautious in our choice of companions. Choose people with characteristics you would like to develop in your own life.

• **22:26** This verse is saying that it is wise to be slow to countersign a note or to be liable for another person's debt.

22:28 In Joshua 13—21, the land was divided and the boundaries marked out for each tribe. Moses had already warned the people that when they reached the promised land they shouldn't cheat their neighbors by moving one of the landmarks to give themselves more land and their neighbors less (Deuteronomy 19:14; 27:17). "Gerrymandering"—changing political boundaries so that one group of voters benefits and another loses—is a modern form of moving boundary markers.

• **23:1–3** The point of this proverb is to be careful when eating with an influential person, because he may try to bribe you. No good will come from the meal.

23:4,5 Prov 15:27 27:23,24; 28:20 Mt 6:19 1 Tim 6:17

[4]Do not wear yourself out to get rich;
have the wisdom to show restraint.
[5]Cast but a glance at riches, and they are gone,
for they will surely sprout wings
and fly off to the sky like an eagle.

23:6 Prov 1:15; 4:14

[6]Do not eat the food of a stingy man,
do not crave his delicacies;
[7]for he is the kind of man
who is always thinking about the cost.[a]
"Eat and drink," he says to you,
but his heart is not with you.
[8]You will vomit up the little you have eaten
and will have wasted your compliments.

23:9 Prov 14:7; 24:7

[9]Do not speak to a fool,
for he will scorn the wisdom of your words.

23:10 Deut 19:14 27:17 Jer 22:3 Zech 7:10

[10]Do not move an ancient boundary stone
or encroach on the fields of the fatherless,
[11]for their Defender is strong;
he will take up their case against you.

23:12 Prov 2:2; 5:1 22:17

[12]Apply your heart to instruction
and your ears to words of knowledge.

23:13 Prov 13:24 19:18; 29:15 1 Cor 5:5

[13]Do not withhold discipline from a child;
if you punish him with the rod, he will not die.
[14]Punish him with the rod
and save his soul from death.[b]

23:15 Prov 4:1; 10:1 15:20; 27:11

[15]My son, if your heart is wise,
then my heart will be glad;
[16]my inmost being will rejoice
when your lips speak what is right.

23:17 Ps 37:1; 73:3 Prov 24:1,19

[17]Do not let your heart envy sinners,
but always be zealous for the fear of the LORD.
[18]There is surely a future hope for you,
and your hope will not be cut off.

23:19 Prov 20:1; 23:29

[19]Listen, my son, and be wise,
and keep your heart on the right path.

[a] 7 Or *for as he thinks within himself, / so he is*; or *for as he puts on a feast, / so he is* [b] 14 Hebrew *Sheol*

• **23:4, 5** We have all heard of people who have won millions of dollars and then lost it all. Even the average person can spend an inheritance—or a paycheck—with lightning speed and have little to show for it. Don't spend your time chasing fleeting earthly treasures. Instead store up treasures in heaven, for such treasures will never be lost. (See Luke 12:33, 34 for Jesus' teaching.)

• **23:6–8** In graphic language, the writer warns us not to envy the life-styles of those who have become rich by being stingy and miserly, and not to gain their favor by fawning over them. Their "friendship" is phony—they will just use you for their own gain.

23:10, 11 The term *Defender* or *redeemer* refers to someone who bought back a family member who had fallen into slavery or who accepted the obligation to marry the widow of a family member (Ruth 4:3–10). God is also called a Redeemer (Exodus 6:6; Job 19:25). (For an explanation of ancient boundary markers, see the note on 22:28.)

23:12 The people most likely to gain knowledge are those who are willing to listen. It is a sign of strength, not weakness, to pay attention to what others have to say. People who are eager to listen continue to learn and grow throughout their lives. If we refuse to become set in our ways, we can always expand the limits of our knowledge.

23:13, 14 The stern tone of correction here is offset by the affection expressed in verse 15. However, many parents are reluctant to discipline their children at all. Some fear they will forfeit their relationship, that their children will resent them, or that they will stifle their children's development. But discipline won't kill them, and it may prevent them from foolish moves that will.

23:17, 18 How easy it is to envy those who get ahead unhampered by Christian responsibility or God's laws. For a time they do seem to get ahead without paying any attention to God's desires. But to those who follow him, God promises a hope and a wonderful future even if we don't realize it in this life.

[20]Do not join those who drink too much wine
or gorge themselves on meat,
[21]for drunkards and gluttons become poor,
and drowsiness clothes them in rags.

[22]Listen to your father, who gave you life,
and do not despise your mother when she is old.
[23]Buy the truth and do not sell it;
get wisdom, discipline and understanding.
[24]The father of a righteous man has great joy;
he who has a wise son delights in him.
[25]May your father and mother be glad;
may she who gave you birth rejoice!

23:22 Prov 13:1; 15:5 Deut 21:18
23:23 Prov 4:7; 18:15 Mt 13:44
23:24 Prov 10:1; 23:15

[26]My son, give me your heart
and let your eyes keep to my ways,
[27]for a prostitute is a deep pit
and a wayward wife is a narrow well.
[28]Like a bandit she lies in wait,
and multiplies the unfaithful among men.

23:26 Prov 6:26; 22:14 Eccles 7:26

[29]Who has woe? Who has sorrow?
Who has strife? Who has complaints?
Who has needless bruises? Who has bloodshot eyes?
[30]Those who linger over wine,
who go to sample bowls of mixed wine.
[31]Do not gaze at wine when it is red,
when it sparkles in the cup,
when it goes down smoothly!
[32]In the end it bites like a snake
and poisons like a viper.
[33]Your eyes will see strange sights
and your mind imagine confusing things.
[34]You will be like one sleeping on the high seas,
lying on top of the rigging.
[35]"They hit me," you will say, "but I'm not hurt!
They beat me, but I don't feel it!
When will I wake up
so I can find another drink?"

23:29 Prov 20:1; 23:19
23:32 Ps 140:3

24

Do not envy wicked men,
do not desire their company;
[2]for their hearts plot violence,
and their lips talk about making trouble.

[3]By wisdom a house is built,
and through understanding it is established;
[4]through knowledge its rooms are filled
with rare and beautiful treasures.

24:1 Ps 1:1; 37:3 Prov 1:15

23:29, 30 The soothing comfort of alcohol is only temporary. Real relief comes from dealing with the cause of the anguish and sorrow and turning to God for peace. Don't lose yourself in alcohol; find yourself in God.

23:29–35 Israel was a wine-producing country. In the Old Testament, winepresses bursting with new wine were considered a sign of blessing (3:10). Wisdom is even said to have set her table with wine (9:2, 5). But the Old Testament writers were alert to the dangers of wine. It dulls the senses; it limits clear judgment (31:1–9); it lowers the capacity for control (4:17); it destroys one's efficiency (21:17). To make wine an end in itself, a means of self-indulgence, or an escape from life is to misuse it and invite the consequences of the drunkard.

24:5 The athlete who thinks—who assesses the situation and plans strategies—has an advantage over a physically stronger but unthinking opponent. And wisdom, not muscle, is certainly what has put man in charge of the animal kingdom. We exercise regularly and eat well to build our strength; but do we take equal pains to develop wisdom? Because wisdom is a vital part of strength, it pays to attain it.

24:5 Prov 21:22
24:6 Prov 11:14
24:7 Prov 14:6
24:8 Prov 6:14; 14:22
24:10 Job 4:5 Heb 12:3
24:11,12 1 Sam 16:7 Ps 82:4 Eccles 5:8
24:13 Ps 19:10 Prov 25:16
24:15,16 Job 5:19 Ps 10:9-12 Prov 6:15 14:32; 24:21,22
24:17 Ps 35:15 Rom 11:18-21
24:19 Job 15:31 Prov 13:9; 24:1
24:21 Prov 24:15,16 Rom 13:4

5A wise man has great power,
and a man of knowledge increases strength;
6for waging war you need guidance,
and for victory many advisers.

7Wisdom is too high for a fool;
in the assembly at the gate he has nothing to say.

8He who plots evil
will be known as a schemer.
9The schemes of folly are sin,
and men detest a mocker.

10If you falter in times of trouble,
how small is your strength!

11Rescue those being led away to death;
hold back those staggering toward slaughter.
12If you say, "But we knew nothing about this,"
does not he who weighs the heart perceive it?
Does not he who guards your life know it?
Will he not repay each person according to what he has done?

13Eat honey, my son, for it is good;
honey from the comb is sweet to your taste.
14Know also that wisdom is sweet to your soul;
if you find it, there is a future hope for you,
and your hope will not be cut off.

15Do not lie in wait like an outlaw against a righteous man's house,
do not raid his dwelling place;
16for though a righteous man falls seven times, he rises again,
but the wicked are brought down by calamity.

17Do not gloat when your enemy falls;
when he stumbles, do not let your heart rejoice,
18or the LORD will see and disapprove
and turn his wrath away from him.

19Do not fret because of evil men
or be envious of the wicked,
20for the evil man has no future hope,
and the lamp of the wicked will be snuffed out.

21Fear the LORD and the king, my son,
and do not join with the rebellious,
22for those two will send sudden destruction upon them,
and who knows what calamities they can bring?

24:6 In any major decision we make concerning college, marriage, career, children, etc., it is not a sign of weakness to ask for advice. Instead it is foolish not to ask for it. Find good advisers before making any big decision. They can help you expand your alternatives and evaluate your choices.

24:8 Plotting to do evil can be as wrong as doing it because what you think determines what you will do. Left unchecked, wrong desires will lead to sin. God wants lives free from sin; and planning evil spoils the purity even if the act has not yet been committed. Should you say, "Then I might as well go ahead and do it, because I've already planned it"? No. You have sinned in your attitude, but you have not yet damaged other people. Stop in your tracks and ask God to forgive you and put you on a different path.

24:10 Times of trouble can be useful. They show you who you really are, what kind of character you have developed. In addition, they help you grow stronger. When Jeremiah questioned God because of the trouble he faced, God asked how he ever expected to face big challenges if the little ones wore him out (Jeremiah 12:5). Don't complain about your problems. The trouble you face today is training you to be strong for the more difficult situations you will face in the future.

24:17, 18 David, Solomon's father, refused to gloat over the death of his lifelong enemy Saul (see 2 Samuel 1). On the other hand, the nation of Edom rejoiced over Israel's defeat and was punished by God for this (Obadiah 1:12). To gloat over others' misfortune is to make yourself the avenger and to put yourself in the place of God, who alone is the real judge of all the earth (see Deuteronomy 32:35).

Further Sayings of the Wise

[23]These also are sayings of the wise:

To show partiality in judging is not good:
[24]Whoever says to the guilty, "You are innocent"—
peoples will curse him and nations denounce him.
[25]But it will go well with those who convict the guilty,
and rich blessing will come upon them.

[26]An honest answer
is like a kiss on the lips.

[27]Finish your outdoor work
and get your fields ready;
after that, build your house.

[28]Do not testify against your neighbor without cause,
or use your lips to deceive.
[29]Do not say, "I'll do to him as he has done to me;
I'll pay that man back for what he did."

[30]I went past the field of the sluggard,
past the vineyard of the man who lacks judgment;
[31]thorns had come up everywhere,
the ground was covered with weeds,
and the stone wall was in ruins.
[32]I applied my heart to what I observed
and learned a lesson from what I saw:
[33]A little sleep, a little slumber,
a little folding of the hands to rest—
[34]and poverty will come on you like a bandit
and scarcity like an armed man.[a]

24:23
Prov 18:5; 28:21

24:26
Job 6:25
Prov 15:23
25:12; 27:5

24:28,29
Prov 20:22
25:18
Mt 5:39
Rom 12:17

24:30
Job 4:8
Prov 6:6
Isa 5:6,7

24:32
Prov 6:10
12:24; 23:21

C. WISDOM FOR THE LEADERS (25:1—31:31)

These proverbs were collected by Hezekiah's aides. The first section was written by Solomon, and the next two sections were written by others. While we all can learn from these proverbs, many were originally directed toward the king or those who dealt with the king. These are particularly helpful for those who are leaders or aspire to become leaders. The book ends with a description of a truly good wife, who is an example of godly wisdom.

More Proverbs of Solomon

25 These are more proverbs of Solomon, copied by the men of Hezekiah king of Judah:

[2]It is the glory of God to conceal a matter;
to search out a matter is the glory of kings.

25:1
Prov 1:1

25:2
Deut 29:29
Ezra 6:1
Rom 11:33

[a] 34 Or *like a vagrant / and scarcity like a beggar*

24:26 A kiss on the lips was a sign of true friendship. People often think that they should bend the truth to avoid hurting a friend. But one who gives an honest, straightforward answer is a true friend.

• **24:27** We should carry out our work in its proper order. If a farmer builds his house in the spring, he misses the planting season and goes a year without food. If a businessman invests his money in a house while his business is struggling to grow, he may lose both. It is possible to work hard and still lose everything if the timing is wrong or the resources to carry it out are not in place.

24:29 Here is a reverse version of the Golden Rule (see Luke 6:31). Revenge is the way the world operates, but it is not God's way.

25:1 Hezekiah's story is told in 2 Kings 18—20; 2 Chronicles 29—32; and Isaiah 36—39. He was one of the few kings of Judah who honored the Lord. By contrast, his father Ahaz actually nailed the temple door shut. Hezekiah restored the temple, destroyed idol worship centers, and earned the respect of surrounding nations, many of whom brought gifts to God because of him. It is not surprising that Hezekiah had these proverbs copied and read, for "in everything that he undertook in the service of God's temple and in obedience to the law and the commands, he sought his God and worked wholeheartedly. And so he prospered" (2 Chronicles 31:21).

3As the heavens are high and the earth is deep,
so the hearts of kings are unsearchable.

25:4,5
Prov 20:8
Ezek 22:18
Mal 3:2,3

4Remove the dross from the silver,
and out comes material for[a] the silversmith;
5remove the wicked from the king's presence,
and his throne will be established through righteousness.

25:6
Ps 131:1
Prov 25:27; 27:2
Mt 12:39
Lk 14:7

6Do not exalt yourself in the king's presence,
and do not claim a place among great men;
7it is better for him to say to you, "Come up here,"
than for him to humiliate you before a nobleman.

25:8
Prov 17:14; 18:6
Mt 5:25

What you have seen with your eyes
8 do not bring[b] hastily to court,
for what will you do in the end
if your neighbor puts you to shame?

9If you argue your case with a neighbor,
do not betray another man's confidence,
10or he who hears it may shame you
and you will never lose your bad reputation.

25:11
Prov 15:23

11A word aptly spoken
is like apples of gold in settings of silver.

25:12
Prov 15:31

12Like an earring of gold or an ornament of fine gold
is a wise man's rebuke to a listening ear.

13Like the coolness of snow at harvest time
is a trustworthy messenger to those who send him;
he refreshes the spirit of his masters.

14Like clouds and wind without rain
is a man who boasts of gifts he does not give.

25:15
Prov 15:1
Eccles 10:4

15Through patience a ruler can be persuaded,
and a gentle tongue can break a bone.

25:16
Prov 25:27

16If you find honey, eat just enough—
too much of it, and you will vomit.
17Seldom set foot in your neighbor's house—
too much of you, and he will hate you.

25:18
Ps 57:4
Prov 12:18
24:28
Jer 9:8

18Like a club or a sword or a sharp arrow
is the man who gives false testimony against his neighbor.

25:19
Job 6:15

19Like a bad tooth or a lame foot
is reliance on the unfaithful in times of trouble.

25:20
Prov 27:14

20Like one who takes away a garment on a cold day,
or like vinegar poured on soda,
is one who sings songs to a heavy heart.

[a] 4 Or *comes a vessel from* [b] 7,8 Or *nobleman / on whom you had set your eyes. / 8Do not go*

25:6, 7 Jesus made this proverb into a parable (see Luke 14:7–11). We should not seek honor for ourselves. It is better to quietly and faithfully accomplish the work God has given us to do. As others notice the quality of our lives then they will draw attention to us.

25:13 It is often difficult to find people you can really trust. A faithful employee ("messenger") is punctual, responsible, honest, and hardworking. This person is invaluable as he/she helps take some of the pressure off his or her employer. Find out what your employer needs from you to make his or her job easier, and do it.

•**25:14** Most churches, missions organizations, and Christian groups depend on the gifts of people to keep their ministries going. But many who promise to give fail to follow through. The Bible is very clear about the effect this has on those involved in the ministry. If you make a pledge, keep your promise.

25:18 Lying ("false testimony") is vicious. Its effects can be as permanent as those of a stab wound. The next time you are tempted to pass on a bit of gossip, imagine yourself stabbing the victim of your remarks with a sword. This image may shock you into silence.

[21]If your enemy is hungry, give him food to eat;
if he is thirsty, give him water to drink.
[22]In doing this, you will heap burning coals on his head,
and the LORD will reward you.

25:21,22 Ex 23:4; 2 Kgs 6:22; 2 Chron 28:15; Mt 5:44; 6:6; Rom 12:20

[23]As a north wind brings rain,
so a sly tongue brings angry looks.

25:23 Prov 13:3; 26:20

[24]Better to live on a corner of the roof
than share a house with a quarrelsome wife.

25:24 Prov 19:13; 21:9; 27:15

[25]Like cold water to a weary soul
is good news from a distant land.

25:25 2 Cor 7:7; 1 Thess 3:5-8

[26]Like a muddied spring or a polluted well
is a righteous man who gives way to the wicked.

25:26 Ezek 34:18

[27]It is not good to eat too much honey,
nor is it honorable to seek one's own honor.

25:27 Prov 25:16

[28]Like a city whose walls are broken down
is a man who lacks self-control.

26

Like snow in summer or rain in harvest,
honor is not fitting for a fool.

26:1 1 Sam 12:17; Prov 26:8

[2]Like a fluttering sparrow or a darting swallow,
an undeserved curse does not come to rest.

26:2 Num 23:8; 2 Sam 16:12; Ps 109:28

[3]A whip for the horse, a halter for the donkey,
and a rod for the backs of fools!

26:3 Ps 32:9; Prov 10:13

[4]Do not answer a fool according to his folly,
or you will be like him yourself.

26:4 Prov 23:9

[5]Answer a fool according to his folly,
or he will be wise in his own eyes.

[6]Like cutting off one's feet or drinking violence
is the sending of a message by the hand of a fool.

26:6 Prov 13:17; 25:13

[7]Like a lame man's legs that hang limp
is a proverb in the mouth of a fool.

26:7 Ps 50:16,17; Prov 17:7

[8]Like tying a stone in a sling
is the giving of honor to a fool.

25:21, 22 God's form of retaliation is most effective and yet difficult to do. Paul quotes this proverb in Romans 12:19–21. In Matthew 5:44, Jesus encourages us to pray for those who hurt us. By returning good for evil, we're acknowledging God as the balancer of all accounts and trusting him to be the judge.

25:26 To "give way to the wicked" means setting aside your standards of right and wrong. No one is helped by someone who compromises with the wicked.

25:27 Dwelling on the honors you deserve can only be harmful. It can make you bitter, discouraged, or angry, and it will not bring you the rewards you think should be yours. Pining for what you should have received may make you miss the satisfaction of knowing you did your best.

25:28 Even though city walls restricted the inhabitants' movements, people were happy to have them. Without walls, they would have been vulnerable to attack by any passing group of marauders. Self-control limits us, to be sure, but it is necessary. An out-of-control life is open to all sorts of enemy attack. Think of self-control as a wall for defense and protection.

26:2 "An undeserved curse does not come to rest" means that it has no effect.

26:4, 5 These two verses seem to be in contradiction. But the writer is saying that we shouldn't take a foolish person seriously and try to reason with his or her empty arguments. This will only make him or her proud and determined to win the argument. Instead, we should give light and foolish replies.

•**26:7** In the mouth of a fool, a proverb becomes as useless as a paralyzed leg. Some people are so blind that they won't get much wisdom from reading these proverbs. Only those who want to be wise have the receptive attitude needed to make the most of them. If we want to learn from God, he responds and pours out his heart to us (1:23).

26:8 Sometimes when someone in a group causes discord or dissension, the leader tries to make him loyal and productive by giving him a place of privilege or responsibility. This doesn't always work. In fact, it is like tying the stone to the sling – it won't go anywhere and will swing back and hurt you. The dissenter's new power may be just what he needs to manipulate the group.

[9]Like a thornbush in a drunkard's hand
is a proverb in the mouth of a fool.

[10]Like an archer who wounds at random
is he who hires a fool or any passer-by.

26:11 Ex 8:15; 2 Pet 2:22

[11]As a dog returns to its vomit,
so a fool repeats his folly.

26:12 Prov 3:7; 28:11

[12]Do you see a man wise in his own eyes?
There is more hope for a fool than for him.

26:13 Prov 15:19

[13]The sluggard says, "There is a lion in the road,
a fierce lion roaming the streets!"

26:14 Prov 6:9; 19:15

[14]As a door turns on its hinges,
so a sluggard turns on his bed.

26:15 Prov 12:27; Eccles 4:5

[15]The sluggard buries his hand in the dish;
he is too lazy to bring it back to his mouth.

[16]The sluggard is wiser in his own eyes
than seven men who answer discreetly.

26:17 Prov 3:30; 18:6

[17]Like one who seizes a dog by the ears
is a passer-by who meddles in a quarrel not his own.

26:18,19 Prov 24:12,28

[18]Like a madman shooting
firebrands or deadly arrows
[19]is a man who deceives his neighbor
and says, "I was only joking!"

THE FOUR TONGUES
What we say probably affects more people than any other action we take. It is not surprising, then, to find that Proverbs gives special attention to words and how they are used. Four common speech patterns are described in Proverbs. The first two should be copied, while the last two should be avoided.

Tongue	Description	References
The Controlled Tongue	Those with this speech pattern think before speaking, know when silence is best, and give wise advice.	10:19; 11:12, 13; 12:16; 13:3; 15:1, 4, 28; 16:23; 17:14, 27–28; 21:23; 24:26
The Caring Tongue	Those with this speech pattern speak truthfully while seeking to encourage.	10:32; 12:18, 25; 15:23; 16:24; 25:15; 27:9
The Conniving Tongue	Those with this speech pattern are filled with wrong motives, gossip, slander, and twist truth.	6:12–14; 8:13; 16:28; 18:8; 25:18; 26:20–28
The Careless Tongue	Those with this speech pattern are filled with lies, curses, quick-tempered words—which can lead to rebellion and destruction.	10:18, 32; 11:9; 12:16, 18; 15:4; 17:9, 14, 19; 20:19; 25:23

Other verses about our speech include: 10:11, 20, 31; 12:6, 17–19; 13:2; 14:3; 19:5, 28; 25:11; 27:2, 5, 14, 17; 29:9

26:9 Normally the first prick of a thorn alerts us, and we remove the thorn before it damages us. A drunk person, however, may not feel the thorn, and so it works its way into his flesh. Similarly, a fool may not feel the sting of a proverb, because he does not see where it touches his life. Instead of taking its point to heart, a fool will apply it to his church, his employer, his spouse, or whomever he is rebelling against. The next time you find yourself saying, "So-and-so should really pay attention to that," stop and ask yourself—"Is there a message in it for me?"

26:13–16 If a person is not willing to work, he can find endless excuses to avoid it. But laziness is more dangerous than a prowling lion. The less you do, the less you want to do, and the more useless you become. To overcome laziness, take a few small steps toward change. Set a concrete, realistic goal. Figure out the steps needed to reach it, and follow those steps. Pray for strength and persistence. To keep your excuses from making you useless, stop making useless excuses.

26:17 Seizing the ears of a stray dog is a good way to get bitten, and interfering in arguments is a good way to get hurt. Many times both arguers will turn on the person who interferes. It is best simply to keep out of arguments that are none of your business. If you must become involved, try to wait until the arguers have stopped fighting and cooled off a bit. Then maybe you can help them mend their differences and their relationship.

[20]Without wood a fire goes out;
without gossip a quarrel dies down.

26:20 Prov 16:28 Jas 3:6

[21]As charcoal to embers and as wood to fire,
so is a quarrelsome man for kindling strife.

26:21 Prov 10:12 15:18; 29:22

[22]The words of a gossip are like choice morsels;
they go down to a man's inmost parts.

26:22 Prov 18:8; 20:19

[23]Like a coating of glaze[a] over earthenware
are fervent lips with an evil heart.

26:23 Mt 23:28 Lk 11:39

[24]A malicious man disguises himself with his lips,
but in his heart he harbors deceit.
[25]Though his speech is charming, do not believe him,
for seven abominations fill his heart.
[26]His malice may be concealed by deception,
but his wickedness will be exposed in the assembly.

26:24 Prov 12:20

[27]If a man digs a pit, he will fall into it;
if a man rolls a stone, it will roll back on him.

26:27 Ps 7:15

[28]A lying tongue hates those it hurts,
and a flattering mouth works ruin.

27

Do not boast about tomorrow,
for you do not know what a day may bring forth.

27:1 Mt 6:34 Lk 12:19,20 Jas 4:13-16

[2]Let another praise you, and not your own mouth;
someone else, and not your own lips.

27:2 Prov 25:27 2 Cor 10:12,18

[3]Stone is heavy and sand a burden,
but provocation by a fool is heavier than both.

[4]Anger is cruel and fury overwhelming,
but who can stand before jealousy?

27:4 Prov 6:34

[5]Better is open rebuke
than hidden love.

27:5 Prov 24:26 25:12; 28:23

[6]Wounds from a friend can be trusted,
but an enemy multiplies kisses.

27:6 Ps 141:5 Mt 26:49

[7]He who is full loathes honey,
but to the hungry even what is bitter tastes sweet.

[8]Like a bird that strays from its nest
is a man who strays from his home.

27:8 Prov 21:16

[9]Perfume and incense bring joy to the heart,
and the pleasantness of one's friend springs from his earnest
counsel.

[10]Do not forsake your friend and the friend of your father,
and do not go to your brother's house when disaster strikes you—
better a neighbor nearby than a brother far away.

27:10 1 Kgs 12:6 2 Chron 10:6 Prov 17:17

[a] 23 With a different word division of the Hebrew; Masoretic Text *of silver dross*

26:20 Talking about every little irritation or piece of gossip only keeps the fires of anger going. Refusing to discuss them cuts the fuel line and makes the fires die out. Does someone continually irritate you? Decide not to complain about the person, and see if your irritation dies from lack of fuel.

26:24–26 This proverb means that a man with hate in his heart may sound pleasant enough, but don't believe what he says.

27:6 Who would prefer a friend's wounds to an enemy's kisses? Anyone who considers the source. A friend who has your best interests at heart may have to give you unpleasant advice at times, but you know it is for your own good. An enemy, by contrast, may whisper sweet words and happily send you on your way to ruin. We tend to hear what we want to hear, even if an enemy is the only one who will say it. A friend's advice, no matter how painful, is much better.

27:11 Prov 10:1; 23:15

[11]Be wise, my son, and bring joy to my heart;
then I can answer anyone who treats me with contempt.

27:12 Prov 22:3

[12]The prudent see danger and take refuge,
but the simple keep going and suffer for it.

27:13 Prov 6:1-5

[13]Take the garment of one who puts up security for a stranger;
hold it in pledge if he does it for a wayward woman.

27:14 Prov 26:18,19

[14]If a man loudly blesses his neighbor early in the morning,
it will be taken as a curse.

27:15 Prov 19:13 21:9; 25:24

[15]A quarrelsome wife is like
a constant dripping on a rainy day;
[16]restraining her is like restraining the wind
or grasping oil with the hand.

[17]As iron sharpens iron,
so one man sharpens another.

27:18 Lk 12:42 2 Tim 2:6

[18]He who tends a fig tree will eat its fruit,
and he who looks after his master will be honored.

[19]As water reflects a face,
so a man's heart reflects the man.

27:20 Prov 30:15 Eccles 1:8-11 Hab 2:5

[20]Death and Destruction[a] are never satisfied,
and neither are the eyes of man.

27:21 1 Sam 18:7,8 2 Sam 14:25 Ps 12:6 Prov 17:3 Zech 13:9 Lk 6:26

[21]The crucible for silver and the furnace for gold,
but man is tested by the praise he receives.

27:22 Prov 26:11 Jer 5:3

[22]Though you grind a fool in a mortar,
grinding him like grain with a pestle,
you will not remove his folly from him.

27:24 Job 19:9

[23]Be sure you know the condition of your flocks,
give careful attention to your herds;
[24]for riches do not endure forever,
and a crown is not secure for all generations.
[25]When the hay is removed and new growth appears
and the grass from the hills is gathered in,
[26]the lambs will provide you with clothing,
and the goats with the price of a field.

[a] *20* Hebrew *Sheol and Abaddon*

27:15, 16 Quarrelsome nagging, a steady stream of unwanted advice, is a form of torture. People nag because they think they're not getting through, but nagging hinders communication more than it helps. When tempted to engage in this destructive habit, stop and examine your motives. Are you more concerned about yourself—getting your way, being right—than about the person you are pretending to help? If you are truly concerned about other people, think of a more effective way to get through to them. Surprise them with words of patience and love, and see what happens.

27:17 There is a mental sharpness that comes from being around good people. And a meeting of minds can help people see their ideas with new clarity, refine them, and shape them into brilliant insights. This requires discussion partners who can challenge each other and stimulate thought—people who focus on the idea without involving their egos in the discussion, people who know how to attack the thought and not the thinker. Two friends who bring their ideas together can help each other become sharper.

• **27:18** With all the problems and concerns a leader has, it can be easy to overlook the very people who most deserve attention—faithful employees or volunteers (those who tend the fig trees). The people who stand behind you, who work hard and help you get the job done, deserve to share in your success. Be sure that in all your worrying, planning, and organizing, you don't forget the people who are helping you the most.

27:21 Praise tests a person, just as high temperatures test metal. How does praise affect you? Do you work to get it? Do you work harder after you've gotten it? Your attitude toward praise tells a lot about your character. People of high integrity are not swayed by praise. They are attuned to their inner convictions, and they do what they should whether or not they are praised for it.

• **27:23–27** Because life is short and our fortunes uncertain, we should be all the more diligent in what we do with our lives. We should act with foresight, giving responsible attention to our homes, our families, and our careers. We should be responsible stewards, like a farmer with his lands and herds. Thinking ahead is a duty, not an option, for God's people.

[27]You will have plenty of goats' milk
to feed you and your family
and to nourish your servant girls.

28

The wicked man flees though no one pursues,
but the righteous are as bold as a lion.

28:1 Ps 27:1,2

[2]When a country is rebellious, it has many rulers,
but a man of understanding and knowledge maintains order.

28:2 1 Kgs 16:8-28; 2 Kgs 15:8-15; Hos 7:7; 8:4

[3]A ruler[a] who oppresses the poor
is like a driving rain that leaves no crops.

[4]Those who forsake the law praise the wicked,
but those who keep the law resist them.

28:4 Rom 1:32

[5]Evil men do not understand justice,
but those who seek the LORD understand it fully.

28:5 Ps 92:6,7; Prov 2:9; 21:15

[6]Better a poor man whose walk is blameless
than a rich man whose ways are perverse.

28:6 Prov 12:9

[7]He who keeps the law is a discerning son,
but a companion of gluttons disgraces his father.

28:7 Prov 23:25,26; 29:3

[8]He who increases his wealth by exorbitant interest
amasses it for another, who will be kind to the poor.

28:8 Ex 22:25; Deut 23:19,20

[9]If anyone turns a deaf ear to the law,
even his prayers are detestable.

28:9 Ps 66:18; 109:7; Prov 15:8

[10]He who leads the upright along an evil path
will fall into his own trap,
but the blameless will receive a good inheritance.

28:10 Prov 26:27; Mt 5:19; 18:6

[11]A rich man may be wise in his own eyes,
but a poor man who has discernment sees through him.

28:11 Prov 18:23; 26:12

[12]When the righteous triumph, there is great elation;
but when the wicked rise to power, men go into hiding.

[13]He who conceals his sins does not prosper,
but whoever confesses and renounces them finds mercy.

28:13 Ps 32:1-11; 1 Jn 1:6-9

[a] 3 Or *A poor man*

28:2 For a government or a society to endure, it needs wise, informed leaders—and these are hard to find. "It has many rulers" means that anarchy is prevailing. Each person's selfishness quickly affects others. A selfish employee who steals from his company ruins its productivity. A selfish driver who drinks before taking the wheel makes the state highways unsafe. A selfish spouse who has an adulterous affair often breaks up several families. When enough people live for themselves with little concern for how their actions affect others, the resulting moral rot contaminates the entire nation. Are you part of the problem . . . or the solution?

28:5 Because justice is part of God's character, a person who follows God treats others justly. The beginning of justice is concern for what is happening to others. A Christian cannot be indifferent to human suffering because God isn't. And we certainly must not contribute to human suffering through selfish business practices or unfair government policies. Be sure you are more concerned for justice than for the bottom line.

•**28:9** God does not listen to our prayers if we intend to go back to our sin as soon as we get off our knees. If we want to forsake our sin and follow him, however, he willingly listens—no matter how bad our sin has been. What closes his ears is not the depth of our sin, but our secret intention to do it again.

•**28:11** Rich people often think they are wonderful; depending on no one, they take credit for all they do. But that's a hollow self-esteem. Through dependence on God in their struggles, the poor may develop a richness of spirit that no amount of wealth can provide. The rich man can lose all his material wealth, while no one can take away the poor man's character. Don't be jealous of the rich; money may be all they will ever have.

•**28:13** It is human nature to hide our sins or overlook our mistakes. But it is hard to learn from a mistake you don't acknowledge making. And what good is a mistake if it doesn't teach you something? To learn from an error you need to admit it, confess it, analyze it, and make adjustments so that it doesn't happen again. Everybody makes mistakes, but only fools repeat them.

•**28:13** Something in each of us strongly resists admitting we are wrong. That is why we admire people who openly and graciously admit their mistakes and sins. These people have a strong self-image. They do not always have to be right to feel good about themselves. Be willing to reconsider—to admit you are wrong and to change your plans when necessary. And remember, the first step toward forgiveness is confession.

28:14 Rom 2:5 Phil 2:12

[14]Blessed is the man who always fears the LORD,
but he who hardens his heart falls into trouble.

28:15 Prov 19:12 Mt 2:16 1 Pet 5:8

[15]Like a roaring lion or a charging bear
is a wicked man ruling over a helpless people.

28:16 Eccles 10:16 Isa 3:12

[16]A tyrannical ruler lacks judgment,
but he who hates ill-gotten gain will enjoy a long life.

28:17 Gen 9:6 Ex 21:14 Prov 6:16-19 28:24

[17]A man tormented by the guilt of murder
will be a fugitive till death;
let no one support him.

[18]He whose walk is blameless is kept safe,
but he whose ways are perverse will suddenly fall.

28:19 Prov 12:11 14:4; 23:19-21

[19]He who works his land will have abundant food,
but the one who chases fantasies will have his fill of poverty.

[20]A faithful man will be richly blessed,
but one eager to get rich will not go unpunished.

[21]To show partiality is not good—
yet a man will do wrong for a piece of bread.

[22]A stingy man is eager to get rich
and is unaware that poverty awaits him.

28:23 Ps 141:5 Prov 29:5,6 Mt 18:15

[23]He who rebukes a man will in the end gain more favor
than he who has a flattering tongue.

DILIGENCE AND LAZINESS
Proverbs makes it clear that diligence—being willing to work hard and do one's best at any job given to him or her—is a vital part of wise living. We work hard not to become rich, famous, or admired (although those may be by-products), but to serve God with our very best during our lives.

The Diligent	*The Lazy*	*References*
Become rich	Are soon poor	10:4
Gather crops early	Sleep during harvest	10:5
	Are an annoyance	10:26
Have abundant food	Chase fantasies	12:11
Hard work returns rewards		12:14
Will rule	Will become slaves	12:24
Prize his possessions	Waste good resources	12:27
Are fully satisfied	Want much but get little	13:4
Bring profit	Experience poverty	14:23
Have an easy path	Have trouble all through life	15:19
	Are like those who destroy	18:9
	Go hungry	19:15
	Won't feed themselves	19:24
	Won't plow in season	20:4
Stay awake and have food to spare	Love sleep and grow poor	20:13
Are steady plodders	Make hasty speculations	21:5
	Love pleasure and become poor	21:17
Give without sparing	Desire things but refuse to work for them	21:25, 26
	Are full of excuses for not working	22:13
Will serve before kings		22:29
	Sleep too much, which leads to poverty	24:30–34
Reap prosperity through hard work	Experience poverty because of laziness	28:19

28:17, 18 A sinner's conscience will drive him either into guilt resulting in repentance, or to death itself because of a refusal to repent. It is no act of kindness to try to make him feel better; the more guilt he feels, the more likely he is to turn to God and repent. If we interfere with the natural consequences of his act, we may make it easier for him to continue in sin.

[24]He who robs his father or mother
and says, "It's not wrong"—
he is partner to him who destroys.

28:24
Prov 19:26

[25]A greedy man stirs up dissension,
but he who trusts in the LORD will prosper.

[26]He who trusts in himself is a fool,
but he who walks in wisdom is kept safe.

28:26
Job 28:28
Prov 3:5

[27]He who gives to the poor will lack nothing,
but he who closes his eyes to them receives many curses.

28:27
Prov 11:24
19:17

[28]When the wicked rise to power, people go into hiding;
but when the wicked perish, the righteous thrive.

29

A man who remains stiff-necked after many rebukes
will suddenly be destroyed—without remedy.

29:1
Prov 1:24,25
13:18; 15:31,32

[2]When the righteous thrive, the people rejoice;
when the wicked rule, the people groan.

29:2
Esth 8:15,16
Prov 11:10

[3]A man who loves wisdom brings joy to his father,
but a companion of prostitutes squanders his wealth.

29:3
Prov 6:26; 10:1
Lk 15:13

[4]By justice a king gives a country stability,
but one who is greedy for bribes tears it down.

29:4
Prov 8:15

[5]Whoever flatters his neighbor
is spreading a net for his feet.

29:5
Ps 5:9
Prov 28:23

[6]An evil man is snared by his own sin,
but a righteous one can sing and be glad.

[7]The righteous care about justice for the poor,
but the wicked have no such concern.

29:7
Ps 41:1

[8]Mockers stir up a city,
but wise men turn away anger.

29:8
Prov 13:2; 17:19
Jas 3:13-18

[9]If a wise man goes to court with a fool,
the fool rages and scoffs, and there is no peace.

[10]Bloodthirsty men hate a man of integrity
and seek to kill the upright.

[11]A fool gives full vent to his anger,
but a wise man keeps himself under control.

29:11
Prov 14:17,29

[12]If a ruler listens to lies,
all his officials become wicked.

28:26 For many people, the rugged individualist is a hero. We admire the bold, self-directed men and women who know what they want and fight for it. They are self-reliant, neither giving nor asking advice. What a contrast to God's way. A person can't know the future and can't predict the consequences of his choices with certainty. And so the totally self-reliant person is doomed to failure. The wise person depends on God.

28:27 God wants us to identify with the needy, not ignore them. The second part of this proverb could be restated positively: "those who open their eyes to poor people will be blessed." If we help others when they are in trouble, they will do whatever they can to return the favor (see 11:24, 25). Paul promises that God will supply all our needs (Philippians 4:19); he does this through other people. What can you do today to help God supply someone's need?

29:1 Making the same mistake over and over is an invitation to disaster. Eventually people have to face the consequences of refusing to learn. If their mistake is refusing God's invitations or rejecting his commands, the consequences will be especially serious. In the end, God may have to turn them away. Make sure you are not stiff-necked.

29:13 "The LORD gives sight to the eyes of both" means everyone depends on God for sight. Both the oppressor and the poor have the gift of sight from the same God. God sees and judges both, and his judgment falls on those whose greed or power drives them to oppress the poor.

29:13
Prov 22:2

[13]The poor man and the oppressor have this in common:
The LORD gives sight to the eyes of both.

29:14
Ps 72:4
Prov 16:12; 29:4

[14]If a king judges the poor with fairness,
his throne will always be secure.

[15]The rod of correction imparts wisdom,
but a child left to himself disgraces his mother.

29:16
Ps 37:34-38

[16]When the wicked thrive, so does sin,
but the righteous will see their downfall.

[17]Discipline your son, and he will give you peace;
he will bring delight to your soul.

29:18
Ex 32:25
Ps 1:1,2; 74:9

[18]Where there is no revelation, the people cast off restraint;
but blessed is he who keeps the law.

[19]A servant cannot be corrected by mere words;
though he understands, he will not respond.

29:20
Prov 26:12

[20]Do you see a man who speaks in haste?
There is more hope for a fool than for him.

[21]If a man pampers his servant from youth,
he will bring grief[a] in the end.

29:22
Prov 22:24

[22]An angry man stirs up dissension,
and a hot-tempered one commits many sins.

29:23
Prov 15:33; 22:4
Dan 4:30

[23]A man's pride brings him low,
but a man of lowly spirit gains honor.

29:24
Prov 1:10,11

[24]The accomplice of a thief is his own enemy;
he is put under oath and dare not testify.

[a] *21* The meaning of the Hebrew for this word is uncertain.

LEADERSHIP
Since many of the proverbs came from King Solomon, it is natural to expect some of his interest to be directed toward leadership.

Qualities of good leadership	*References*
Diligence	12:24
Trustworthy messengers	13:17
Don't penalize people for integrity	17:26
Listen before answering	18:13
Open to new ideas	18:15
Listen to both sides of the story	18:17
Able to stand under adversity	24:10
Able to stand under praise	27:21
What happens without good leadership	
Honoring the wrong people backfires	26:8
A wicked ruler is dangerous	28:15
People despair	29:2
A wicked ruler has wicked aides	29:12

Other verses to study: 24:27; 25:13; 27:18

29:15 As parents of young children, we weary of disciplining them. It seems that all we do is nag, scold, and punish. When you're tempted to give up and let them do what they want, or when you wonder if you've ruined every chance for a loving relationship with them, remember—kind, firm discipline helps them learn, and learning makes them wise. Consistent, loving discipline will ultimately teach them to discipline themselves.

29:16 In any organization—whether a church, a business, a family, or a government—the climate comes from the top. The people become like their leaders. What kind of climate are you setting for the people you lead?

29:18 "Revelation" refers to words from God received by prophets. Where there is ignorance of God, crime and sin run wild. Public morality depends on the knowledge of God, but it also depends on keeping God's laws. In order for both nations and individuals to function well, people must know God's ways and keep his rules.

29:24 This proverb is saying that a thief's accomplice won't tell the truth when under oath. Thus, by his perjury, he hurts himself.

[25]Fear of man will prove to be a snare,
but whoever trusts in the LORD is kept safe.

[26]Many seek an audience with a ruler,
but it is from the LORD that man gets justice.

[27]The righteous detest the dishonest;
the wicked detest the upright.

29:25 Prov 16:7

29:27 Mt 10:22; 24:9 2 Cor 6:14-18

Sayings of Agur

30 The sayings of Agur son of Jakeh — an oracle[a]:

This man declared to Ithiel,
to Ithiel and to Ucal:[b]

[2]"I am the most ignorant of men;
I do not have a man's understanding.
[3]I have not learned wisdom,
nor have I knowledge of the Holy One.
[4]Who has gone up to heaven and come down?
Who has gathered up the wind in the hollow of his hands?
Who has wrapped up the waters in his cloak?
Who has established all the ends of the earth?
What is his name, and the name of his son?
Tell me if you know!

[5]"Every word of God is flawless;
he is a shield to those who take refuge in him.
[6]Do not add to his words,
or he will rebuke you and prove you a liar.

[7]"Two things I ask of you, O LORD;
do not refuse me before I die:
[8]Keep falsehood and lies far from me;
give me neither poverty nor riches,
but give me only my daily bread.
[9]Otherwise, I may have too much and disown you
and say, 'Who is the LORD?'
Or I may become poor and steal,
and so dishonor the name of my God.

[10]"Do not slander a servant to his master,
or he will curse you, and you will pay for it.

[11]"There are those who curse their fathers
and do not bless their mothers;

30:2 Job 42:3-6

30:4 Job 26:8 Ps 24:2; 68:18 Isa 45:18

30:5 Ps 3:3; 12:6 18:30; 84:11

30:6 Deut 4:2; 12:32 Rev 22:18

30:9 Deut 8:12; 31:20 Neh 9:25 Hos 13:6

30:10 Eccles 7:21

30:11 Ex 21:17 Prov 20:20

[a] 1 Or *Jakeh of Massa* [b] 1 Masoretic Text; with a different word division of the Hebrew *declared, "I am weary, O God; / I am weary, O God, and faint.*

• **29:25** Fear of people can hamper everything you try to do. In extreme forms, it can make you afraid to leave your home. By contrast, fear of God – respect, reverence, and trust – is liberating. Why fear people who can do no eternal harm? Instead, fear God who can turn the harm intended by others into good for those who trust him.

30:1 The origin of these sayings is not clear. Nothing is known about Agur except that he was a wise teacher who may have come from Lemuel's kingdom (see the note on 31:1).

30:2–4 Because God is infinite, certain aspects of his nature will always remain a mystery. Compare these questions with the questions God asked Job (Job 38 – 41).

• **30:4** Some scholars feel that the son referred to is the Son of God, the preincarnate being of the Messiah who, before the foundation of the earth, participated in the creation. Colossians 1:16, 17 teaches that through Christ the world was created.

30:7–9 Having too much money can be dangerous, but so can having too little. Being poor can, in fact, be hazardous to spiritual as well as physical health. On the other hand, being rich is not the answer. As Jesus pointed out, rich people have trouble getting into God's kingdom (Matthew 19:23, 24). Like Paul, we can learn how to live whether we have little or plenty (Philippians 4:12), but our lives are more likely to be effective if we have "neither poverty nor riches."

30:13,14
Job 29:17
Ps 57:4
Lk 18:11

30:15,16
Gen 30:1,2
Prov 27:20

30:17
Gen 9:22
Prov 19:26
20:20

30:18,19
Job 39:27; 42:3
Ps 139:6

30:20
Prov 7:13

30:22
1 Sam 25:25
Ps 14:1
Prov 17:7,21

30:24,25
Job 12:7-9
Prov 6:6-8

30:26
Lev 11:5
Ps 104:18

[12]those who are pure in their own eyes
and yet are not cleansed of their filth;
[13]those whose eyes are ever so haughty,
whose glances are so disdainful;
[14]those whose teeth are swords
and whose jaws are set with knives
to devour the poor from the earth,
the needy from among mankind.

[15]"The leech has two daughters.
'Give! Give!' they cry.

"There are three things that are never satisfied,
four that never say, 'Enough!':
[16]the grave,[a] the barren womb,
land, which is never satisfied with water,
and fire, which never says, 'Enough!'

[17]"The eye that mocks a father,
that scorns obedience to a mother,
will be pecked out by the ravens of the valley,
will be eaten by the vultures.

[18]"There are three things that are too amazing for me,
four that I do not understand:
[19]the way of an eagle in the sky,
the way of a snake on a rock,
the way of a ship on the high seas,
and the way of a man with a maiden.

[20]"This is the way of an adulteress:
She eats and wipes her mouth
and says, 'I've done nothing wrong.'

[21]"Under three things the earth trembles,
under four it cannot bear up:
[22]a servant who becomes king,
a fool who is full of food,
[23]an unloved woman who is married,
and a maidservant who displaces her mistress.

[24]"Four things on earth are small,
yet they are extremely wise:
[25]Ants are creatures of little strength,
yet they store up their food in the summer;
[26]coneys[b] are creatures of little power,
yet they make their home in the crags;
[27]locusts have no king,
yet they advance together in ranks;
[28]a lizard can be caught with the hand,
yet it is found in kings' palaces.

[29]"There are three things that are stately in their stride,
four that move with stately bearing:

[a] *16* Hebrew *Sheol* [b] *26* That is, the hyrax or rock badger

•**30:13** This phrase refers to prideful and haughty people who look down on others. Verses 11–14 contain a fourfold description of arrogance.

30:15ff "Three things . . . four" is a poetic way of saying the list is not complete. The writer of these proverbs is observing the world with delighted interest. Verses 15–30 are an invitation to look at nature from the perspective of a keen observer.

•**30:24–28** Ants can teach us about preparation; coneys (badgers) about wise building; locusts about cooperation and order; and lizards about fearlessness.

[30]a lion, mighty among beasts,
who retreats before nothing;
[31]a strutting rooster, a he-goat,
and a king with his army around him.[a]

[32]"If you have played the fool and exalted yourself,
or if you have planned evil,
clap your hand over your mouth!
[33]For as churning the milk produces butter,
and as twisting the nose produces blood,
so stirring up anger produces strife."

30:30 Prov 20:2 Mic 5:8
30:32 Job 21:5; 40:4 Prov 17:27,28 Mic 7:16
30:33 Prov 15:18 16:28; 26:21 29:22

Sayings of King Lemuel

31 The sayings of King Lemuel—an oracle[b] his mother taught him:

[2]"O my son, O son of my womb,
O son of my vows,[c]
[3]do not spend your strength on women,
your vigor on those who ruin kings.

[4]"It is not for kings, O Lemuel—
not for kings to drink wine,
not for rulers to crave beer,
[5]lest they drink and forget what the law decrees,
and deprive all the oppressed of their rights.
[6]Give beer to those who are perishing,
wine to those who are in anguish;
[7]let them drink and forget their poverty
and remember their misery no more.

[8]"Speak up for those who cannot speak for themselves,
for the rights of all who are destitute.
[9]Speak up and judge fairly;
defend the rights of the poor and needy."

31:3 Prov 5:9; 7:26
31:4 Prov 20:1 Eccles 10:16,17
31:5 Deut 16:19 Prov 17:15
31:8 Job 29:12-17

Epilogue: The Wife of Noble Character

[10][d]A wife of noble character who can find?
She is worth far more than rubies.
[11]Her husband has full confidence in her
and lacks nothing of value.
[12]She brings him good, not harm,
all the days of her life.
[13]She selects wool and flax
and works with eager hands.

31:10 Ruth 3:11 Prov 8:11; 12:4
31:11 1 Pet 3:1,2
31:13 Gen 18:6 24:18-20

[a] 31 Or *king secure against revolt* [b] 1 Or *of Lemuel king of Massa, which* [c] 2 Or */ the answer to my prayers*
[d] 10 Verses 10-31 are an acrostic, each verse beginning with a successive letter of the Hebrew alphabet.

31:1 Little is known about Lemuel except that he was a king who received wise teachings from his mother. His name means "devoted to God." It is believed that Lemuel and Agur were both from the kingdom of Massa in northern Arabia.

• **31:4–7** Drunkenness might be understandable among dying people in great pain, but it is inexcusable for national leaders. Alcohol clouds the mind and can lead to injustice and poor decisions. Leaders have better things to do than anesthetize themselves with alcohol.

• **31:10–31** Proverbs has a lot to say about women. How fitting that the book ends with a picture of a woman of strong character, great wisdom, many skills, and great compassion.

Some people have the mistaken idea that the ideal woman in the Bible is retiring, servile, and entirely domestic. Not so! This woman is an excellent wife and mother. She is also a manufacturer, importer, manager, realtor, farmer, seamstress, upholsterer, and merchant. Her strength and dignity do not come from her amazing achievements, however. They are a result of her reverence for God. In our society where physical appearance counts for so much, it may surprise us to realize that her appearance is never mentioned. Her attractiveness comes entirely from her character.

The woman described in this chapter has outstanding abilities. Her family's social position is high. In fact, she may not be one woman at all—she may be a composite portrait of ideal womanhood. Do not see her as a model to imitate in every detail; your days are not long enough to do everything she does! See her instead as an inspiration to be all you can be. We can't be just like

14She is like the merchant ships,
bringing her food from afar.
15She gets up while it is still dark;
she provides food for her family
and portions for her servant girls.
16She considers a field and buys it;
out of her earnings she plants a vineyard.
17She sets about her work vigorously;
her arms are strong for her tasks.
18She sees that her trading is profitable,
and her lamp does not go out at night.
19In her hand she holds the distaff
and grasps the spindle with her fingers.
20She opens her arms to the poor
and extends her hands to the needy.
21When it snows, she has no fear for her household;
for all of them are clothed in scarlet.
22She makes coverings for her bed;
she is clothed in fine linen and purple.
23Her husband is respected at the city gate,
where he takes his seat among the elders of the land.
24She makes linen garments and sells them,
and supplies the merchants with sashes.
25She is clothed with strength and dignity;
she can laugh at the days to come.
26She speaks with wisdom,
and faithful instruction is on her tongue.
27She watches over the affairs of her household
and does not eat the bread of idleness.
28Her children arise and call her blessed;
her husband also, and he praises her:
29"Many women do noble things,
but you surpass them all."
30Charm is deceptive, and beauty is fleeting;
but a woman who fears the LORD is to be praised.
31Give her the reward she has earned,
and let her works bring her praise at the city gate.

31:20 Deut 15:11 Job 31:16 Prov 22:9 Rom 12:13

31:22 Ps 45:13,14 Ezek 16:9,10

31:23 Job 29:7

31:25 Prov 14:26

31:26 Prov 11:16

31:27 Prov 6:6-11

31:30 Prov 1:7; 8:13

31:31 Ps 128:2,3

---

her, but we can learn from her industry, integrity, and resourcefulness.

31:19 The distaff and spindle are two implements used in hand spinning.

• **31:31** The book of Proverbs begins with the command to fear the Lord (1:7) and ends with the picture of a woman who fulfills this command. Her qualities are mentioned throughout the book: hard work, fear of God, respect for spouse, foresight, encouragement, care for others, concern for the poor, wisdom in handling money. These qualities, when coupled with fear of God, lead to enjoyment, success, honor, and worth. Proverbs is very practical for our day because it shows us how to become wise, make good decisions, and live according to God's ideal.

HOW TO USE THIS BIBLE STUDY

It's always exciting to get more than you expect. And that's what you'll find in this Bible study guide—much more than you expect. Our goal was to write thoughtful, practical, dependable, and application-oriented studies of God's Word.

This study guide contains the complete text of the selected Bible book. The commentary is accurate, complete, and loaded with unique charts, maps, and profiles of Bible people.

With the Bible text, extensive notes and helps, and questions to guide discussion, these Life Application Study Guides have everything you need in one place.

The lessons in this Bible study guide will work for large classes as well as small-group studies. To get everyone involved in your discussions, encourage participants to answer the questions before each meeting.

Each lesson is divided into five easy-to-lead sections. The section called "Reflect" introduces you and the members of your group to a specific area of life touched by the lesson. "Read" shows which chapters to read and which notes and other features to use. Additional questions help you understand the passage. "Realize" brings into focus the biblical principle to be learned with questions, a special insight, or both. "Respond" helps you make connections with your own situation and personal needs. The questions are designed to help you find areas in your life where you can apply the biblical truths. "Resolve" helps you map out action plans for that day.

Begin and end each lesson with prayer, asking for the Holy Spirit's guidance, direction, and wisdom.

Recommended time allotments for each section of a lesson:

Segment	**60 minutes**	**90 minutes**
Reflect on your life	5 minutes	10 minutes
Read the passage	10 minutes	15 minutes
Realize the principle	15 minutes	20 minutes
Respond to the message	20 minutes	30 minutes
Resolve to take action	10 minutes	15 minutes

All five sections work together to help a person learn the lessons, live out the principles, and obey the commands taught in the Bible.

Also, at the end of each lesson, there is a section entitled "More for studying other themes in this section." These questions will help you lead the group in studying other parts of each section not covered in depth by the main lesson.

Do not merely listen to the word, and so deceive yourselves. Do what it says. Anyone who listens to the word but does not do what it says is like a man who looks at his face in a mirror and, after looking at himself, goes away and immediately forgets what he looks like. But the man who looks intently into the perfect law that gives freedom, and continues to do this, not forgetting what he has heard, but doing it—he will be blessed in what he does. (James 1:22-25, NIV)

LESSON 1
THE MARKS OF WISE LIVING
PROVERBS 1:1-7

REFLECT
on your life

1 Describe one of the wisest persons you know (point out at least three characteristics of wisdom in his/her life).

2 How do you think he/she became wise?

READ
the passage

Read the introduction to Proverbs, the chart "Understanding Proverbs" on page 5, Proverbs 1:1-7, and the following notes:

❐1:1 ❐1:7 ❐1:7-9

3 For what reasons did Solomon write and collect these proverbs?

4 Which of the three types of proverbs described in the chart has been used in one of these verses?

REALIZE
the principle

The wisdom in Proverbs affects every part of life. All actions are marked by wisdom's presence or absence. In fact, wisdom is seen more clearly in the *way* we live and work than in what we do. Students, bakers, bankers, and homemakers all do what they do with more or less wisdom. Every stage of life, from childhood to old age, can be evaluated by the number of wise or foolish decisions that have been made. You need the wisdom of Proverbs today. It begins with acknowledging God's right to be the center of your life. It continues as you allow him to direct every other part of your life.

5 What characteristics of wisdom and discipline would make fools despise both those qualities?

RESPOND
to the message

6 Give some examples of fears that have been helpful to you. Using the note on 1:7, why is fearing the Lord the beginning of knowledge?

7 What do verbs like *attaining, acquiring,* and *giving* tell you about the way wisdom enters a person's life?

8 A number of purposes for Proverbs have been given in these opening verses. List them below.

Purposes	Rating		
a ______	H	M	L
b ______	H	M	L
c ______	H	M	L
d ______	H	M	L
e ______	H	M	L

9 Use your list of purposes for Proverbs to give a personal importance rating for each of them. Assign a high, medium, or low rating for each according to its importance right now in your life.

10 Choose one of your highly rated purposes and explain your reasons for giving it that rating.

______

______

______

______

11 What events or people has God used in the past to help increase or expand your wisdom?

______

______

______

______

RESOLVE
to take action

12 Finish the following sentence as it applies to you. I will have grown in wisdom when I note the following changes in the way I live:

______

______

______

______

______

13 Whom do you know who already has the qualities you desire? Decide on a time when you can ask them how they learned that aspect of wisdom. Pause and ask God to use this part of his Word to grow your wisdom.

MORE
for studying other themes in this section

A Read various proverbs to test your ability to identify the different types listed in the Special Features section of Vital Statistics. Which are the most difficult for you to identify?

B Why would it be a good idea for anyone who wants to learn more about the Bible to memorize Proverbs 1:7?

C What is the difference between the common definition of wisdom as the accumulation of knowledge and the Biblical view of wisdom as a skillful way to see and live?

LESSON 2
WISDOM'S BENEFITS
PROVERBS 1:8—4:27

REFLECT
on your life

1 From the following list of job perks and benefits, which five would you choose as the most appealing? Circle your top five.

medical insurance

office with a window

personal days

expense account

reimbursing education

profit sharing

advancement opportunities

company car

conferences at vacation spots

pension plan

disability insurance

dental coverage

scheduled raises

bonuses

2 Besides the items just discussed, what other significant factors make a job desirable?

READ
the passage

Study the chart "Wisdom: Applied Truth" on page 9, then read Proverbs 1:8—4:27 and the following notes:

❏1:8 ❏1:22 ❏1:31, 32 ❏2:9, 10 ❏3:6 ❏3:16, 17 ❏4:5-7

3 In what places can wisdom be found? Why do so many people miss it?

4 What specific benefits of wisdom, or wise living, did you discover in 1:8—4:27?

5 Based on these chapters, what relationships are affected by wisdom?

6 What are the main characteristics of someone who rejects wisdom? What are the consequences of that rejection? List at least five of each.

7 Are people more likely to chose wisdom because of its benefits or because of the consequences of rejecting it? Why?

REALIZE
the principle

Experiments on selective attention have been conducted on crowded street corners. The assortment of sounds is deafening as vehicles rush by and the crowd shuffles back and forth. Tempers flare and horns honk. But if a coin is dropped on the sidewalk, the monetary jingle seems to catch everyone's ear. Many in our society are tuned in to that sound. Their attentiveness is a measure of what is really important to them.

Likewise, we can be "tuned in" to wisdom. It can become so important that we are liable to find it everywhere. Wisdom grows in those who watch, listen and look for her. Being alert to wisdom is itself a wise way to live. Proverbs notes many of the distractions which can keep us from wisdom, but it also points out that those who trust in the source of wisdom and make their goal to obey him hear wisdom's voice even on busy street corners.

8 What situation in your life could most be described as your "busy street corner" where you need to hear wisdom in spite of the noise?

RESPOND to the message

9 Using the chart "Wisdom: Applied Truth," what connection is there between certain benefits of wisdom and certain characteristics of wisdom? For instance, how does the fact that a wise person is loving lead to the benefits of a long, prosperous life?

10 Which benefit of wisdom offers you the strongest motivation to make it a higher priority than it is in your life right now?

11 What have been the most consistent sources of wisdom in your own life?

12 Describe some mistakes you've made that have turned out to teach you wisdom.

13 In what decision-making areas do you find yourself wanting greater wisdom (refer to Proverbs 3:5, 6)? When did you last ask God specifically for wisdom in those areas?

14 Choose at least one decision where you need wisdom and at least one situation where you need to discover the wise way of action. Take time to pray for the wisdom you need for each of these.

RESOLVE
to take action

15 Choose one of the proverbs regarding the benefits of wisdom and memorize it this week. Look for three examples around you of how wisdom has benefited others.

MORE
for studying
other themes
in this section

A Make a list of all the synonyms used for wisdom in these chapters. What are other words you use to describe wisdom?

B Read Proverbs 2:1-6. What is our role and God's role in gaining wisdom?

C Read Proverbs 3:5, 6 and the note. How does godly wisdom help us approach planning and goal setting?

D How do the principles found in Proverbs 3:9, 10 relate to your thinking on Sunday mornings as the offering plate is passed in church?

E How does the principle of discipline found in Proverbs 3:11, 12 fit into your relationship with God?

F What does Proverbs 4:1-4 teach about parent-child relationships?

G Although friendships are important, what limits are placed on them by Proverbs 4:14-16?

H What types of guarding does Proverbs 4:27 refer to in relation to the heart?

LESSON 3
WISE MOVES
PROVERBS 5:1—7:27

REFLECT
on your life

1 Describe a few of the ways in which society's standards of morality have changed in your lifetime.

2 What are the strongest influences on sexual values in society today?

READ
the passage

Read Proverbs 5:1—7:27 and the following notes:

❒5:3 ❒5:3-8 ❒5:11-13 ❒5:15 ❒5:15-21 ❒5:18-20 ❒6:25 ❒6:25-35 ❒7:6-23 ❒7:25-27

3 Alongside the advice concerning sexual activity, what other areas of morality are mentioned in these chapters? (Note specially Proverbs 6:16-19).

4 How does Proverbs 5:21 provide a key standard for personal convictions on moral issues?

5 Based on the figurative language in Proverbs (such as 5:15-19; 6:25-29; 7:21-23), what is a Biblical attitude towards sexual morality?

6 What are the reasons given in these chapters for maintaining sexual purity and strong convictions?

7 How do people in our society tend to react to these reasons?

8 Why is sexuality such a troublesome area for Christians?

REALIZE
the principle

One of the characteristics of the sinful nature in humans is our tendency to live on the edge of evil. Instead of finding ways to stay as far as possible from those things which can cause us to fall, we want to know just how close we can come without really getting in trouble. We try to decide what is right and wrong from moment to moment instead of basing decisions on convictions which we have gotten from God's Word. Instant morality rarely resists sin, but God's Word provides a wise escape.

Proverbs never denies the powerful attractiveness of sin. Wisdom realizes that putting ourselves in situations where we experience the attraction of sin is dangerous. Getting close to sin makes it very difficult to see the consequences beyond the immediate temptation. In cases of attractive sin, the best resistance is avoidance.

The standards described in Proverbs may seem unrealistic to Christians who have already violated them. Sin needs to be recognized, but the reality of forgiveness must also be proclaimed. Seeking God's forgiveness can be the beginning of new convictions.

9 How do human responses like repentance, confession, and asking God for forgiveness fit with verses like Proverbs 6:23?

10 Recognizing that we have different levels of resistance to certain sins, how should we handle the difference in personal convictions that will come when we honestly apply God's Word?

RESPOND
to the message

11 Describe several of your strongest personal convictions and explain how you came to hold them.

12 In what one area of your life do you need clearly understood convictions? How will you develop these convictions?

13 What responsibilities does God give to adults to help young people develop strong moral convictions?

14 What actions could you take to help at least one young person maintain sexual purity?

15 What challenges to your personal convictions do you expect to encounter this week? How will you respond?

RESOLVE
to take action

16 Think of a young person for whom you could pray specifically about his or her moral purity. Write or call to tell him or her you are praying God will help him or her develop strong convictions.

MORE
for studying other themes in this section

A In what ways is Proverbs 5:11-14 a strong case for developing convictions when we are young?

B Read Proverbs 6:1-5 and its note. How does having wisdom apply to personal loans and sharing responsibility for debt?

C Compare the responsibilities of children and parents found in Proverbs 6:20-23.

D If convictions are defined as a personal plan for acting on God's wisdom in our lives, how might different Christians develop personal applications of Proverbs 6:27, 28 in areas like videos, friendships, or entertainment?

LESSON 4
PLAYING THE FOOL
PROVERBS 8:1—9:18

REFLECT
on your life

1 Who would you nominate in the categories of wisest and most foolish cartoon characters in the comic strips today?

______

______

______

2 Describe something foolish you have done that would have made an ideal episode in a comic strip.

______

______

______

______

READ
the passage

Study the chart "Wisdom and Foolishness" on page 27, then read Proverbs 8:1—9:18 and the following notes:

❒8:1ff ❒9:1ff ❒9:7-10 ❒9:14-17

3 How did God use wisdom in his work of creation as described in Proverbs 8:22-31?

______

______

______

4 Using Proverbs 9:1-18, create a chart which compares and contrasts the actions and attitudes of Wisdom and Folly.

	Wisdom	Folly
actions		
attitudes		

5 From your readings, write a summary description which completes this statement: "A wise person is someone whose most important goal is . . ."

6 From your readings, write a summary description which completes this statement: "A foolish person is someone whose most important goal is . . ."

7 Why do you agree or disagree with the saying "Once a fool, always a fool"?

REALIZE the principle

Most of us can think of people we would consider wise who, nevertheless, made foolish decisions. The compiler of Proverbs himself, Solomon, although very wise, made very foolish decisions. How can this be?

Wisdom is more than knowing what to do. It also involves doing what we know. The way of foolishness appeals to our desires for power, for pleasure, and for plenty. Most foolish decisions are attempts to gain one or more of the above quickly. Such opportunities need the "second opinion" of wisdom. Wisdom requires that we have better reasons than gaining power, pleasure, or plenty as the basis for decisions.

The difference between the wise and the foolish is how much is put into practice. The wise are constantly becoming more and more at home in Wisdom's house and less at home in Folly's shack.

8 What would Solomon recommend as a first step for anyone realizing they have made a foolish decision?

RESPOND
to the message

9 What message does Wisdom have for the fool in each of us? (Note Proverbs 8:4, 17, 34-36; 9:4, 6)

10 Turn to the chart "Wisdom and Foolishness." Measure yourself by marking a (+) or a (-) between the two columns at each characteristic, depending on which side you recognize in your life. Total your pluses and minuses for an idea of your progress in wisdom.

11 Describe at least one situation where you usually find yourself making foolish decisions (for example, a slick sales pitch, an ad for a movie, sweepstakes entries). What would have to change in order for you to handle this weakness better?

12 List one weak area where you tend to act foolishly. Think of other people you might ask who have faced a similar situation and have had success in resisting or avoiding these.

RESOLVE
to take action

13 Thank God for the good qualities of wisdom that he has helped you develop and ask him for help in specific areas where you know you need to grow.

MORE
for studying
other themes
in this section

A How might a person keep true to the principles stated in Proverbs 8:13?

B Using the note on 8:22-31, look up the other Bible references and compare the statements of John and Paul with Solomon's words. Whose words are most persuasive to you?

C What are some of the strongest visual images, similar to Proverbs 9:1, that you remember from your study of Proverbs? Why are certain visual images easy to remember?

D Read the description of the banquet described by Jesus in Luke 14:15-24 and compare it with Wisdom's banquet in Proverbs 9:1-5.

LESSON 5
GETTING CONTROL OF YOURSELF
PROVERBS 10:1—12:28

REFLECT
on your life

1 What are some jobs or responsibilities that require an unusually high level of personal discipline?

2 Describe an occasion when you observed another person exercise great self-control. What impressed you most about this?

READ
the passage

Study the chart "Diligence and Laziness" on page 57, then read Proverbs 10:1—12:28 and the following notes:

❐ 10:4, 5 ❐ 10:18 ❐ 11:9 ❐ 11:19 ❐ 11:22

3 Find proverbs in this reading that illustrate how self-control affects each of these areas of life:

Conversation

Relationships

Learning

Work

Future

4 What specific directions do you find in chapter ten that would help an undisciplined person develop self-control?

5 In the chart "Diligence and Laziness," how many of the qualities of either type are immediately achieved and how many are gradually achieved?

6 What habits mentioned in these verses do you think most clearly indicate a lack of self-control?

7 Why does it take so long to develop self-control?

REALIZE
the principle

There is an obvious regularity to life. One day follows another; the seasons come and go; each year ushers in the next. But within this sameness, there is infinite variety. No two days are the same. Every one of them is unique, filled with new opportunities to taste life!

Among these opportunities are daily challenges to our present level of self-control and exercises which can allow self-control to grow. In noting the various areas of life that are affected by discipline, you can see that the process is ongoing. Each day finds us in new situations and relationships that require our response. For those committed to growing, even mistakes are transformed into lessons for improved self-control.

8 To what extent is discipline a process and self-control a product in the life of a person who is becoming wise?

9 What qualities would you expect to find in the life of someone who has become a disciplined person?

RESPOND
to the message

10 What mistakes have helped you develop self-control?

11 What areas in your life would change the most if you exercised self-control in them?

12 List three changes a very wise person would make if he/she took over your job.

13 List three changes you think a very wise person might recommend that you make at home.

14 What is keeping you from exercising greater self-control in your home or on the job?

RESOLVE
to take action

15 Be wiser for the next twenty-four hours by asking God to help you to exercise self-control for one day in one of those specific areas you listed above.

MORE
for studying other themes in this section

A Read Proverbs 10:3 and its note. What are some ways that the general truths of Proverbs can be used in a person's life.

B Based on verses like Proverbs 10:9, 10, what should make us think twice before taking sin lightly?

C Compare Proverbs 11:14 with Proverbs 10:21. Is it more wise to be interested in the quantity or the quality of advice that we use in making decisions? Why?

D What kind of interaction is being described by Proverbs 11:9? How have you or your family been harmed by this?

E What does it mean to be an established person? How is the word *established* used in Proverbs 12:3?

F According to Proverbs 12:28, what is a great argument for living a wise life?

LESSON 6
PRIVATE LIVES
PROVERBS 13:1—15:33

REFLECT
on your life

1 List three people who have a reputation for having sound moral principles, and who are honest, upright, and sincere.

____

____

____

2 Which of the following would you choose as the best test for integrity: how a person (1) acts at home, (2) handles success, (3) manages money, (4) fills out income tax forms, or (5) writes in a personal journal?

____

____

____

____

READ
the passage

Study the chart "Honesty and Dishonesty" on page 41, then read Proverbs 13:1—15:33 and the following notes:

❑13:6 ❑13:10 ❑13:19 ❑14:12 ❑15:17-19 ❑15:28

3 What is the relationship between wisdom and integrity?

____

____

____

____

4 In what ways does righteousness guard "the man of integrity"? (See Proverbs 13:6.)

5 What does it cost to be a person of integrity? (Compare to the note on 15:17-19.)

6 From the chart "Honesty and Dishonesty," what is the most compelling reason for you to be more honest?

7 Why do so many people tend to act differently when nobody is looking?

REALIZE
the principle

Although we think of integrity as part of a person's reputation, real integrity begins in private. The real person comes out when it seems as if no one is looking. Are we the same kind of people in the open that we are behind closed doors?

We call the management of public reputations "PR." What we must not forget is that God always knows the "RP"—the real person. The Bible makes it clear that the things we can never hide from God are things we can't even hide from people for long. In spite of the best personal PR, eventually there will be those who really know us. Usually, they will be the people who are also the most important to us. Do we really want them to discover that we are not at all in private what we seem to be like in public?

8 How does a child learn honesty? How does an adult learn honesty?

9 In what ways can the church be a place for all people to learn integrity?

RESPOND
to the message

10 Why is integrity such a rare quality among people today?

11 What does "living with integrity" mean to you? (Refer to the use of the word *integrity* in Proverbs 10:9; 11:3; 13:6; 17:26; and 29:10.)

12 In what areas of your life do you face the biggest challenges to being honest, upright, and sincere?

RESOLVE
to take action

13 What could you do in the next couple of weeks to improve your integrity level?

14 Approach a few people whose integrity you respect and ask them to tell you their opinion of what's important for developing this quality in life.

MORE
for studying other themes in this section

A Choose a proverb from chapter 13 which you think best describes the benefits of obeying God's Word.

B Read Proverbs 13:20 and its note. What are the best sources of advice a person can hope to find?

C How would a verse like Proverbs 13:23 motivate someone to be involved on behalf of social justice?

D According to Proverbs 13:24, why is parental discipline important? What are the limits of that discipline?

E Read Proverbs 14:4 and its note. Identify one or more areas of your own life where you've discovered this truth.

F In what ways should a person double-check a "way that seems right," as in Proverbs 14:12?

G Use the note on Proverbs 14:31 to do a brief study on God's attitude toward the poor and those who oppress them.

LESSON 7
SPEAK UP
PROVERBS 16:1—18:24

REFLECT
on your life

1 What compliments have you received recently? List two or three here.

2 What have you said recently that you wish you could take back?

READ
the passage

Study the chart "The Four Tongues" on page 53, then read Proverbs 16:1—18:24 and the following notes:

❑16:1 ❑16:2 ❑17:5 ❑17:22 ❑17:27, 28 ❑18:8

3 What were the main characteristics of speaking wisely you noted in chapter 16?

4 What were the main characteristics of unwise speech in the same chapter?

5 While observing the silence advised in Proverbs 17:28, what else should people who know they are not yet wise be doing?

6 Why is gossip described this way in Proverbs 18:8?

7 In what ways is the word *heart* used in these chapters?

8 On the chart "The Four Tongues," which speech patterns remind you of something that you said recently?

REALIZE
the principle

While most people would like to be known for having controlled and caring speech patterns, the conniving and careless tongue seems to come more naturally. Apparently, the "forked tongue" has four tines.

The real problem is not with our speeches, but with the speaker. Proverbs 16:23 reminds us that "a wise man's heart guides his mouth." What we say and how we say it are ways of showing who we truly are. Working to change bad habits of speech is an indication of our change of heart. But we need God's help in order to change both inwardly and outwardly. The heart of the tongue problem is in our hearts.

9 What other examples in these chapters indicate that the way we speak is an extension of who we are on the inside? (See Proverbs 16:10, 13, 27.)

RESPOND
to the message

10 What two specific heart changes are noted in Proverbs 18:12 and 18:15?

11 How is Proverbs 18:20, 21 a vivid summary of the effects of wise speech?

12 Roughly what percentage of all your conversation falls into each of the four kinds of speech patterns?

Controlled	______ %	Caring	______ %
Conniving	______ %	Careless	______ %

13 Identify at least one negative habit of speech, such as complaining, criticizing, or ridiculing, that you would like to change.

14 In the next hour, what three positive verbal actions, such as giving encouragement or compliments, could you take towards people?

RESOLVE
to take action

MORE
for studying other themes in this section

A Based on Proverbs 16:3, what is the difference between committing our efforts to the Lord and not committing our efforts to the Lord?

B According to Proverbs 16:4, why is God patient with our evil actions in this life?

C In what area of your life are you most likely to confront the issue of honesty and fairness? What help does Proverbs 16:11 give you?

D Use Proverbs 16:31 to brainstorm positive comments which you could make to the elderly around you.

E Proverbs 17:17 and 18:24 have been used to define both human friendships and the friendship God offers us through Christ. Why would a friendship with Christ be called the ultimate friendship?

F How would the decision-making outline in the note for Proverbs 18:13, 15, 17 have made a difference in the last big decision you made?

LESSON 8
LEARNING TO TEACH
PROVERBS 19:1—22:16

REFLECT
on your life

1 Name one of your favorite teachers and explain what difference he/she made in your life.

____

____

____

____

2 Describe an unusual learning experience from your childhood.

____

____

____

READ
the passage

Study the chart "Teaching and Learning" on page 23, then read Proverbs 19:1—22:16 and the following notes:

❐19:16 ❐19:25 ❐20:4 ❐21:11,12 ❐22:6 ❐22:15

3 Of the actions of wise learners in the "Teaching and Learning" chart, which do you think is the most difficult for students? Which comes the most naturally for you?

____

____

____

4 In the chart "Teaching and Learning," three proverbs give advice to teachers. Which one most closely describes the teacher you mentioned in the answer to the first question? Why?

5 How is self-respect connected with the willingness to learn (See Proverbs 19:8, 16)?

6 What aspects of the teaching role of parents and the learning role of children are noted in Proverbs 19:18, 27; 22:6, 15?

7 How is suffering connected with learning (See Proverbs 19:25; 20:30; and 21:11)?

8 Why do some people refuse to learn? What are some of the consequences of this attitude?

REALIZE
the principle

Our physical survival depends on our ability to learn. As babies and little children, we learn before we realizing we are being taught. Those early lessons can be excellent gifts. But they may also be lasting wounds, and we may need God's special help to unlearn old lessons and habits. God wants to teach us. He designed us to live with him forever, and he wants to help us every way he can. Even if that means relearning major lessons of life.

Sometimes, we can choose our teachers. When the teacher is given to us, we still must decide to be open to learning. We also learn informally from those who aren't official teachers. Because we are learning constantly, we should carefully evaluate who is really teaching us and what we are learning.

9 Note the column "Foolish Failures" in the "Teaching and Learning" chart. What happens when people resist the lessons God brings into their lives?

RESPOND
to the message

10 How can you tell if you have chosen good teachers?

11 Who have you chosen to teach you something over the past year or so?

12 From whom have you learned something valuable by seeing their example or talking with them?

13 What would you most like people to learn from watching and hearing you?

RESOLVE
to take action

14 Who has been an effective spiritual teacher in your life over the past year? What could you do to express your appreciation to that person this week?

15 To help you become a better teacher, ask God to help you become more aware of the ways that your life is influencing others.

MORE
for studying other themes in this section

A Use the large chart "Righteousness and Wickedness" on pages 42 and 43 to review some of the lessons you have learned so far in Proverbs.

B How would Proverbs 19:2 and 21:2 help someone who found himself rationalizing wrong decisions?

C What does it mean to fear the Lord (See Proverbs 19:23, for example)?

D In what areas of life do you find yourself tempted to prove something? How might Proverbs 20:3 counteract your temptation?

E How do the principles mentioned in the note for Proverbs 20:25 affect the way you make promises to God?

F In what ways do Proverbs 21:20 and 22:7 contradict the typical view on how money should be handled?

G Turn to the chart "People Called 'Wise' in the Bible" on page 7. From the list, whom you would most want to join you for a small group learning experience? Why did you choose those people?

LESSON 9
GET RICH!
PROVERBS 22:17—24:34

REFLECT
on your life

1 How much money do you think people need before they can call themselves rich?

2 What would be the very first thing you would do (after paying taxes, of course) if you inherited a large sum of money?

READ
the passage

Study the chart "God's Advice about Money" on page 21, then read Proverbs 22:17—24:34 and the following notes:

❐22:26 ❐23:1-3 ❐23:4, 5 ❐23:6-8 ❐24:27

3 According to Proverbs 22:22, 23 and 23:10, 11, why is it dangerous to cheat the poor?

4 According to Proverbs 23:4-8, what are the dangers of riches?

5 What important principles of money management are the basis of Proverbs 22:26, 27 and 24:27, 32-34?

6 In what ways do Christians regularly fail to follow the wisdom of Proverbs 23:17 in regards to wealth?

7 How do most people learn personal financial management?

REALIZE
the principle

In our world, the most accurate autobiographies are recorded in checkbooks. There a person's priorities are written down in a black-and-white, dollars-and-cents evaluation of what is important. We may be thankful that our financial affairs are usually private, but we must remember that God knows every detail and every motive for how we handle money.

Because money is a necessary part of daily life, it also can become an almost unavoidable temptation. At the same time, it can be a helpful reminder of what God wants us to consider important. The discipline of resisting frivolous expenses and instead investing and giving wisely can help us grow and be closer to God. Each time we record another chapter in our checkbooks, we should remember that God holds us responsible for how we use what he has given us.

8 What role should the church have in teaching people how to handle money?

RESPOND
to the message

9 Of the eight points listed in the chart "God's Advice about Money," which are you doing relatively well? Which do you feel that you are failing or doing relatively poorly?

10 In your opinion, what is responsible use of a credit card?

11 When might it be permissible to vouch for the credit of another person, or to countersign a bank loan for a relative or family member? When would it be wrong?

12 How much should a person try to save? Can saving for the future show a lack of faith, or can failure to save show a lack of faith? Why?

13 What could you do to handle your money more wisely? To whom could you turn for advice?

14 How closely does your checkbook align with your desired level of obedience to God?

RESOLVE
to take action

15 What specific regular expense could be changed to reflect your desire to please God?

MORE
for studying other themes in this section

A What does the expression "apply your heart" mean to you as it is used in Proverbs 22:17 and 23:12?

B How is Proverbs 22:29 an effective encouragement in the pursuit of excellence?

C What principles and warnings regarding the use of alcohol can be found in Proverbs 23:30-35?

D What picture is being painted in Proverbs 24:3, 4?

E What frequent rationalization about not helping others is destroyed by Proverbs 24:11, 12?

LESSON 10
PLANNING TO PLAN
PROVERBS 25:1—27:27

REFLECT
on your life

1 When a coach talks about a game plan, what is he talking about?

2 Besides sports, where else are game plans used?

READ
the passage

Read Proverbs 25:1—27:27 including the following notes:

❐ 25:14 ❐ 26:7 ❐ 27:18 ❐ 27:23-27

3 How does God intervene in the plans that people make? (See Proverbs 16:1-3, 9.)

4 What is the temptation that comes with careful planning? (See Proverbs 27:1.)

5 Of what use is a good plan in the hand of a fool? (See Proverbs 26:7)

6 What is the danger of planning without doing?

REALIZE
the principle

7 What is the danger of doing without planning?

Plans without action are wasted monuments to human creativity. Actions without plans are aimless human activities. And doing both without including God can be fruitless and frustrating efforts.

Among these three mistakes, leaving God out has the most devastating results.

Not only does his Word provide tremendous wisdom in directing both plans and actions, but acknowledging his presence also establishes an attitude of dependence and reminds us that he is ultimately in control of our lives. Leaving God out causes us to rely too heavily on our own wisdom and abilities.

8 How do we know when we have over-planned or under-planned?

9 Name one of God's requirements that you know will take planning in order to obey.

RESPOND
to the message

10 What are some ways that you can acknowledge God in the planning and doing process?

11 How should we respond when we have followed God's directions but the plans and actions haven't turned out as we expected?

12 How much time each week do you spend planning? How much would you like to spend?

13 What are some barriers or interruptions to your planning process?

14 How would better planning or more time spent planning improve your life, family, church, or work? How would this help you to be a better servant of God?

15 Plan to plan. Decide on a regular time each week when you can do some personal planning. When is the best time for you to plan for the coming week?

RESOLVE
to take action

MORE
for studying
other themes
in this section

A How have you seen the truth of Proverbs 25:21-22 proven in your own life?

B In Proverbs 25:24, what are the practical applications for both marriage partners?

C What actual effects are being pictured by the "muddied spring or a polluted well" of Proverbs 25:26?

D What do verses like Proverbs 25:6; 26:12; 27:2, 21 teach about the nature of honor?

E According to Proverbs 26:13-16, what are the main characteristics of a lazy person?

F What aspects of friendship are illustrated by Proverbs 27:6 and 27:17?

LESSON 11
GREAT EXPECTATIONS
PROVERBS 28:1—29:27

REFLECT
on your life

1 Imagine that you are a news reporter on a busy city corner with the assignment to ask the passersby to describe a "righteous person." What do people say?

2 How can you tell whether or not a person is successful?

READ
the passage

Study the chart "How to Succeed in God's Eyes" on page 39, then read Proverbs 28:1—29:27 and the following notes:

❐ 28:9 ❐ 28:11 ❐ 28:13 ❐ 28:26 ❐ 29:25

3 What two types of success are being contrasted in Proverbs 28:6, 11, 27?

4 What corrective does Proverbs 28:26 bring to the saying "To succeed in life, you have to believe in yourself"?

5 How do godly people respond to sins and mistakes in their lives? (See Proverbs 28:13.)

6 What does it take to be a success in God's eyes?

REALIZE
the principle

Many Christians want to succeed in life, but earthly success and godly success are very different. Earthly success looks for the praise of human beings; godly success looks for the pleasure of God. Earthly success is fragile and short-lived; godly success is for eternity. Earthly success is achieved by only a few; godly success is possible for anyone willing to respond to God's love and direction.

Those who set out to achieve earthly success will find nothing more than that. Those who allow God to define their success will sometimes find a measure of earthly success thrown in as an extra. But, compared to the glory of God's pleasure, earthly success is only a small decoration.

7 Why is success in God's eyes better than success in the eyes of the world?

RESPOND
to the message

8 How many of the qualities listed as positive in the chart "How to Succeed in God's Eyes" would be considered qualities for success to your friends?

9 What do you hope to accomplish with your life?

10 If anything were possible, what would you like to accomplish for God?

RESOLVE
to take action

11 What expectations do you have for life that need to be adjusted?

12 What other people might be good sources of advice as you make these adjustments?

MORE
for studying
other themes
in this section

A How does world political news relate to Proverbs 28:2?

B Why is there such lack of discussion of the justice of God even among people who claim to serve him? (Proverbs 28:5)

C How does Proverbs 29:18 point out the importance of having an authority outside ourselves for finding direction in life?

D When is dreaming and planning good? When is it dangerous? (Proverbs 28:19)

E What does it mean to remain stiff-necked after many rebukes (Proverbs 29:1)? When is it good to be stubborn?

LESSON 12
FOLLOWING AND LEADING
PROVERBS 30:1—31:9

REFLECT
on your life

1 What famous person would you least like to work for? Why?

2 Who is the best supervisor you ever had? Why?

READ
the passage

Read the chart "Leadership" on page 59, Proverbs 30:1—31:9, and the following notes:

❒30:4 ❒30:13 ❒30:24-28 ❒31:4-7

3 What four animals are mentioned in Proverbs 30:24-28? What does each animal symbolize about being a leader or a follower?

4 What specific leadership advice did King Lemuel receive from his mother (see Proverbs 31:1-9)?

5 What examples of a leader's wrong self-serving attitude are given in these two chapters of Proverbs?

6 What principles for being an effective follower are noted in Proverbs 12:24; 13:17; 25:13; 25:19; and 27:18?

7 Why do poor followers so often make poor leaders?

REALIZE
the principle

People who know how to be good followers tend to be good leaders. If fact, if you have never succeeded at following, you will probably not succeed at leading. Leaders and followers can make each other's efforts frustrating or effective. Mutual understanding makes all the difference.

Sooner or later, all leaders fail. Some fall short, others fall apart. Those whose final authority is God recognize their own shortcomings and are not surprised by a human leader's weaknesses. But it is easy to shift our expectation of perfection from God's sovereignty to the frail shoulders of a human leader. It is equally tempting for that leader to think he/she can live up to that level of trust. That combination is a formula for failure.

According to the Bible, both leaders and followers are accountable to God. Leaders are loaned authority for a while. Followers are reminded that one day they may be leaders. The Christian principle has always been that both leaders and followers are servants. They serve God and each other. The only service they are forbidden is self-service.

8 How do new leaders in the church learn how to lead according to Biblical principles?

RESPOND
to the message

9 Which one of the qualities on the "Leadership" chart do you think is most difficult for a leader to maintain?

10 What qualities from the chart do you find missing most often in the workplace?

11 What qualities from the chart do you find missing most often at church?

RESOLVE
to take action

12 In those places where you function under someone else's leadership, what changes would make you a better follower?

13 In areas that you have followers, what changes would make you a better leader?

MORE
for studying other themes in this section

A Discuss Agur's prayer from Proverbs 30:7-9. How would you reduce what you want from God to two items?

B Using Agur's style, what groups of things have you noticed that amaze you, or teach you, or have baffled you?

C In the style of King Lemuel's mother, what short list of important ideas would you want to record for your children?

LESSON 13
WHAT A WOMAN!
PROVERBS 31:10-31

REFLECT
on your life

1 In the past twenty years, what have been the biggest changes in the roles and expectations of women?

2 How have roles and expectations remained the same?

READ
the passage

Read Proverbs 31:10-31 and the following notes:

❐31:10-31 ❐31:31

3 These verses describe a woman of character. What personal strengths does she demonstrate?

4 How does God fit into her busy life?

5 How would this woman be received in today's world?

6 What does it mean for a wife and mother to be wise?

REALIZE the principle

Proverbs began with a woman named Wisdom. The book ends with the description of a wise woman. This woman is an ideal. She represents the variety and flexibility of a woman's capabilities. She is not what every woman should be; she reveals what women can be. She also represents God's challenge to men and women to allow him to give them a fulfilling life.

The way of wisdom is to live every part of life skillfully. Wisdom is not the claim to be able to do everything or know everything. It is a commitment to do what a person can do as skillfully as he or she is able to do it. It is learning to use knowledge effectively. Wisdom rejects mediocrity. It brings skillfulness to work, relationships, marriages, money management, children, knowledge, and the daily aspects of knowing and worshiping God. Wisdom is still calling on the street corners, "How long?"

7 How can an ideal like this be useful?

8 How can it be harmful?

RESPOND to the message

9 Which of the qualities described in this woman's life are universal, equally applicable to both men and women?

10 In what area of your life does her example challenge you the most?

11 In what ways would you like to be more like her right now?

12 In what ways will you need to be more like her five years from now?

13 Review some of the main lessons you have learned in this study of Proverbs. What lessons would you like to keep with you for the rest of your life?

RESOLVE
to take action

14 Choose one or more verses from Proverbs that have become personal favorites. Write them on cards to display in a prominent place to help you memorize them.

MORE
for studying other themes in this section

A In what way does the description of this woman challenge or strengthen the view of women you may have discovered in the church?

B In the Hebrew language, this woman's description is an acrostic: a series of lines whose first letters form a pattern. In this case each letter of the alphabet appears in sequence. Brainstorm an acrostic for your life, using the letters A–E (or another set of letters that spell a meaningful word, perhaps your name), list the five personal qualities of wise living you would most like to see incorporated into your life.